POLICE AUDITING

Second Edition

POLICE AUDITING

Standards and Applications

By

ALLAN Y. JIAO, Ph.D.

CHARLES C THOMAS • PUBLISHER, LTD.
Springfield • Illinois • U.S.A.

Published and Distributed Throughout the World by

CHARLES C THOMAS • PUBLISHER, LTD.
2600 South First Street
Springfield, Illinois 62704

© 2015 by CHARLES C THOMAS • PUBLISHER, LTD.

ISBN 978-0-398-09075-3 (paper)
ISBN 978-0-398-09076-0 (ebook)

First Edition, 1999
Second Edition, 2015

Library of Congress Catalog Card Number: 2015008943

With THOMAS BOOKS *careful attention is given to all details of manufacturing
and design. It is the Publisher's desire to present books that are satisfactory as to their
physical qualities and artistic possibilities and appropriate for their particular use.*
THOMAS BOOKS *will be true to those laws of quality that assure a good name
and good will.*

Printed in the United States of America
MM-R-3

Library of Congress Cataloging-in-Publication Data

Jiao, Allan Y.
    Police auditing : standards and applications / by Allan Y. Jiao. --
Second edition.
        pages cm
    Includes bibliographical references and index.
    ISBN 978-0-398-09075-3 (pbk.) -- ISBN 978-0-398-09076-0 (ebook)
    1. Police--Auditing. I. Title.

HV7935.J53 2015
657'83--dc23
                                                        2015008943

PREFACE

My involvement in police auditing began in 1995 when I was approached by a few municipalities about strategies for responding to audits of their police departments. I served as a member on a municipal budget review task force and later as a chairperson of a city public safety committee to evaluate police responses to a variety of audit recommendations. As a police specialist but new to the field of police auditing, I searched for a book on police audits to guide my work with the police. Although a great amount of information was available on government and corporate auditing, not a single work could be found on police auditing. All I was able to lay my hands on were various police audit reports written on individual police departments and fragmentary writings only marginally related to police auditing.

It became clear to me, as a result of this search, that a book on police auditing was needed. Many police officials I came into contact with in the course of audit evaluation and research also expressed a desire for such a work, which they believed would help them better respond to both expected or unexpected external audits. By the time I wrote the first edition of this book in the late 1990s, I reviewed over 100 police audit reports published in the United States, United Kingdom, and Canada; interviewed dozens of police officials involved in police auditing; and collected numerous audit documents from both public and private sectors, in addition to firsthand information I gathered while being engaged in police audit evaluations. Many years have passed since then. Not only has police auditing become a more common practice, but many changes and developments have also occurred in this field. Consequently, this book reflects my involvement in and contemplation on police auditing as well as my research interest in this area over the years.

This book is aimed at three types of readers. First, it provides police executives and police managers as well as police auditors a timely and necessary workbook for understanding the theories, standards, and practices of police auditing. Second, it serves as a valuable source of information for researchers and academicians who review and evaluate police programs. Third, students in undergraduate and graduate criminal justice programs should be able to use this book to fulfill requirements of those courses that address police budgeting, police accountability, police program evaluations, as well as research methods and data analysis. This book, therefore, is relevant and beneficial to police administrators, academics, and criminal justice students alike. It serves a wide range of readers because police auditing has become a common practice in law enforcement agencies at all levels of government, but there has not been any other book written specifically on this subject.

To allow such a wide range of audience to benefit from this work, I have made every effort to provide a comprehensive view of police auditing by examining the theories, standards, procedures, practices, and evaluations of police audit. The purpose of this detailed coverage is to enable the readers to not only obtain a general understanding of different aspects and types of police audits, but also apply the basic principles of police auditing to their particular agencies. To accomplish this and increase the book's readability, I have combined description of police auditing with discussion of planned change, and integrated standards and procedures of police auditing with principles of social scientific research. I intend to explicate a viable approach to changing or reforming the police, rather than write an accounting textbook or a scientific research report.

Americans have been fascinated with changing the police. The usual goals are to improve the quality of police services, streamline police organization and operations, and reduce police corruption and misconduct. These are viable goals, to be sure, but they often obscure the process through which change should be implemented or carried out. Whether correct procedural requirements are followed, however, often determines the end results of police reforms.

This book clarifies the process of police auditing as a workable approach to bringing about improvements in police organizations. This approach, although similar to other police change programs in terms of goals and purposes, employs a different set of standards and procedures in measuring and evaluating the police. Auditing is analytical, critical, and investigative in nature with an accounting or financial basis and consequence. The systematic collection and analysis of information in the process of police auditing bring it also closer in line with principles of social scientific research. With a good understanding of the auditing process, the police should be able to work more cohesively with police auditors and respond effectively to audit recommendations. Ultimately, they should be able to improve their efficiency and effectiveness in handling funds and resources and meet public demand for police services.

There are two simple reasons why police auditing merits the attention of both practitioners and academicians. First, this exercise meets the need of police administrators to learn about the economy, efficiency, and effectiveness of their operations. Police services are universally provided and police departments are an essential operating unit in almost all local governments. Whether police organizations and programs are functioning economically, efficiently, and effectively is a natural concern of most, if not all, police administrators. Reliable financial and performance information provide police departments with the means to assess the value of management overheads, ensure that resources are directed to priorities, and make certain that commanding officers are held accountable for the quality of their programs. Thorough audits of resource allocation and organizational structure also prevent police organizations from becoming overly bureaucratic and ensure their readiness for meeting new challenges and demands.

Second, police auditing provides an important tool for the public and its elected officials to fulfill their oversight responsibilities. Because police agencies take up the largest single-area expenditure in local governments, police services are an area of great concern to the public and news media. Increasingly, the public questions the value of police services in terms of taxes and resources taxpayers provide to the police. The public may become critical of the police when crime rates are extraordinarily high and when police are unable to meet the demand for services. Police audits answer the questions raised by the public as well as its elected representatives by examining how well the police are using the taxpayers' money and what have been the results of a department's use of the resources made available to it. With an accurate estimate of the cost of the services and an assessment of the results expected from the services, elected officials are able to make better decisions when it comes to appropriating funds for police organizations.

Different from corporate audits, police audits go beyond examining financial and financial-related statements. The development of police auditing over the years indicates that the focus of police audits has shifted from rendering financial opinions only to attesting on performance, management, compliance, controls, and operations. Consequently, many police audits are concerned not only with whether police funds are handled properly or in compliance with laws and regulations, but also whether police organizations have achieved the purposes for which their programs were authorized and funded and have done so economically and efficiently. It is clear that a greater emphasis has been placed on performance evaluations in the field of police auditing. In view of this development, this book addresses not only audits of finance and compliance, but also audits of performances, which focus on examining the results of a police department's expenditure of its resources.

After an introduction of the concepts, purposes, and development of police auditing, this book describes some general issues related to changing the police and discusses police auditing as a potentially viable approach for improving police organization, management, and operations. It illustrates the structure and process of planned change and how they address, through police auditing, the issue of efficiency and effectiveness, and lead to desired changes in police management and operations. The book then examines government auditing standards and procedures applicable to police auditing and explains the importance of meeting these requirements in the auditing process. To provide a realistic look at how police auditing is practiced, the book presents some typical problems police auditors encounter in a variety of police departments. These extant audit cases are usually related to the economy and efficiency of police operations and functions, program results and effectiveness, and compliance with laws and regulations. A relatively recent development in police auditing, the Office of Independent Police Auditor (IPA), which has been established in many cities across the United States, is described in terms of its structure and functions. Since a post-audit evaluation is equally important as an audit itself, two major evaluation approaches, process and outcome evaluation, are discussed; and the Camden Police Audit is presented to illustrate the process and outcome evaluation of a local police audit program. Overall, the entire police auditing process can be regarded as a model of planned change with several interrelated elements, including internal and external pressures, organizational disequilibrium, examination and collection of data, innovative and rational decision-making, development of goals and solutions and alternatives, implementation of audit programs, maintaining and monitoring changes, and outcome evaluation.

In the process of preparing and writing this book, I have been assisted by and benefited from numerous individuals. I'd like to thank Herbert Douglas and Jerome Harris for introducing me to a local police audit and their support and encouragement for completing this book. To the many police auditors in the United States and Great Britain, whose audit reports I have reviewed and cited as case examples, thank you for enriching this manuscript with your empirical insight. Thanks also to numerous police officers in the United States who have provided me with access to their agencies and valuable information for this work. Thanks especially to Chief Robert Pugh, Chief William Hill, Chief Charles Kocher, and many other police officials in and around New Jersey. Finally, I'd like to dedicate this book to all police administrators, police managers, police officers, and police auditors who devote their life to the betterment of police services.

A.Y.J.

CONTENTS

POLICE AUDITING

Chapter 1

INTRODUCTION

A variety of approaches have been used to change, control, and reform the police since the first modern police, the London Metropolitan Police, was established in 1829. Efforts to change the police range from internal affairs investigations, managerial control, new police leadership, to external consultancies, civilian reviews, and government-appointed commissions. What makes police auditing different? Police auditing is no different from these other efforts in terms of goals and purposes, which are to bring about positive changes and improvement in police services. What is different are the process and procedures used in effecting and evaluating the change. All types of auditing are analytical, critical, and investigative in nature with an accounting or financial basis or consequence (Mautz & Sharaf, 1985). As Robert H. Montgomery (1912), author of the first book on auditing in America, stated, auditing is the analytical branch of accountancy. The systematic collection and analysis of information in the audit process bring police auditing close in line with major principles of social scientific research.

This is a book about police auditing and how it can be used to improve police performances. Specifically, the book covers the theories, standards, procedures, practices, and evaluations of police audits. The purpose of such coverage is to enable to the reader to gain a general understanding of different aspects and types of police audits and learn to apply the principles of police auditing to a particular police department. Contrary to what is commonly expected, there are a variety of police audits that range from a single focus on police purchasing to a comprehensive audit aimed at increasing police efficiency and effec-

3

tiveness in an entire agency, including its organizational structure, operations, programs, and administrative services. Depending on the degree of comprehensiveness, police auditing may involve accountants, auditors, police specialists, police administrators, municipal officials, state government officials, and civilian representatives in the auditing process. Viewed as a whole, police auditing embodies a planned and systematic approach to changing the police.

Why Police Auditing?

Police services are almost universally provided and police departments are an essential operating unit of most local governments. Whether a police organization and its programs are functioning economically, efficiently, and effectively is a natural concern of police administrators and city officials. Police auditing meets the need of the government officials and police administrators to know about the economy, efficiency, and effectiveness of police operations. A police department, for instance, may be experiencing some controversy concerning its compliance and economy (Malan, 1988). In this situation, the police department needs updated and objective financial information to management. Auditors provide assurance about that information as well as the systems producing that information (Bowsher, 1994). A police department may also be questioned about its efficiency and effectiveness. In this circumstance, the police need accurate information about their performance level and their potential for improvement. Auditors may determine whether the police are performing at the standard level by comparing productivity of police departments located in cities of similar socioeconomic conditions. Upon finding that a police department is performing significantly below its capacity compared with similar agencies, auditors may recommend drastic measures for improvement in police management, organizational structure, and operating procedures.

Reliable financial and performance information provide police departments with an opportunity to reassess the value of management overheads, ensure that resources are directed in line with priorities, match resources with demands, and increase accountability of commanding officers' quality of service. Thorough audits of resource allocation and organizational structure can also prevent police organizations from becoming overly bureaucratic and increase their readiness for meeting new demands and challenges. Departments that have conducted audits are usually able to create more efficient organizational structure by reducing the proportion of police manpower tied up in administrative functions, run more accountable programs by clarifying functions and objectives, and achieve greater performance by monitoring and evaluation. The police have experienced in recent decades as well as in history a wave of reforms to police internal management, particularly in the areas of organizational structure and patrol operations. Through a fundamental review of organization, police auditing can assure that a police department is as economical, effective, and efficient as it can be in translating public money into quality police services (Audit Commission, 1991).

Police service is also an area of great public and news media concern (Drebin & Brannon, 1990). This concern is directly related to the largest single-area expenditure the police occupy in the local government, approaching half of the general fund budget. Increasingly, the public questions the value of police services in terms of taxes and resources the public provides to the police. The public may become critical of police management and program performance when crime rate is extraordinarily high and when the police are unable to meet the demand for services. The public wants to know what has happened to the tax dollars, what has been accomplished with the public funds, and simply why they cannot get the police protection they feel they rightfully deserve. This questioning grows more intense when a perception of police corruption exists and when residents experience a higher crime rate and stronger fear of criminal victimization.

Because of the large expenditure and universality and necessity of police services, the police should be held accountable to the public and subject to oversight. Police audit provides an important tool for elected officials-city councils or similar bodies-to fulfill their oversight functions. Police auditing answers the questions raised by the public as well as elected representatives by assessing the police use of taxpayers' money and the results of a department's use of the resources made available to it (Brown, Gallagher, & Williams, 1982). By objectively acquiring and evaluating evidence, auditors assess the credibility of the information reported by or obtained from police management. With the information on police performance, auditors determine whether changes in police resources, such as personnel and patrol vehicles, relate to expected outcomes. Based on an accurate estimate of the cost of the services provided and on results expected to be derived from the services, elected officials will be in a better position to appropriate funds for police agencies and make rational funding decisions (Drebin et al., 1990).

It should be pointed out, however, that a police service is unlike a service or product a private business provides to consumers. Police protection is provided to the public in general with no specific or direct measure of the cost and benefit to an individual. And there is no competing entity providing the same public service and thereby generating comparable cost and benefit data (Brown et al., 1982). Because of these reasons, corporate audit approaches, while acceptable for exercising corporate oversight, have been found to be inadequate for answering questions regarding police organizations, programs, or operations (Tierney, 1996). Police audits must go beyond examination of financial and financial-related statements and evaluate police efficiency and effectiveness from a public service perspective. A police audit, therefore, is often referred to as a performance audit or an organizational audit. An organizational audit provides a full report of the state of a police agency, which becomes the basis for organizational design (Mackenzie, 1986).

Traditional Police Auditing

Traditional police audits are primarily concerned with examination of financial statements, financial performance, and statements of cash flows. Similar to corporate auditing, these audits produce information on financial positions and activities, including revenues, expenditures, and balance sheets. The purpose of traditional police auditing is to test an agency's disbursement and record-keeping procedures for potential weaknesses or errors. By correcting these weaknesses and errors, which can be repeated frequently during a long period of time, the police agency is expected to save a significant amount of financial resources (Stone & DeLuca, 1994).

Both internal and external auditors have been involved in traditional police auditing. Internally, a police agency's own accounting or auditing staff, if the agency is large enough, conducts a sample audit, a check of a random sample of purchase vouchers, payroll records, and other records of disbursements, to make sure that all disbursements are made and recorded properly. If any serious discrepancies are found, the accounting or auditing staff may conduct an audit of the entire year's records (Lee & Johnson, 1983). Externally, independent CPA firms, under a government contract, are engaged in financial statement audits of police activities. Like the internal accounting or auditing staff in a police agency, independent CPAs also focus on examining and evaluating police accounting records.

To detect discrepancies and errors, traditional police auditors assess specific procedures, programs, or policies in a police department. Some scrutinize a department's procedures for handling of cash and valuables from the time received or obtained to the time of dispersal. Some test the appropriateness of records room procedures, report on a department's training program and promotion policies, investigate a homicide unit's low clearance rate, or review a police chief's authority and accountability. Some audits analyze accuracy of crime data reported to the Federal Bureau of Investigation for its nationwide Uniform Crime Report (UCR) and National Incident-Based Reporting System (NIBRS). Some look at whether members of a detective division have made deliberate effort to lower crime statistics by falsely reporting results of their investigations. Some others study whether use of force guidelines and practices are consistent with laws and government policies, and monitor investigations of complaints against police officers (Auditing and Internal Control Division, 1983a, 1983b; LEN, 1996a, 1996b, 1997a, 1997b, 1997c, 1997d; Walker, 2005).

With the rise of federal assistance to local police agencies in the 1990s, particularly in the area of community-oriented policing, programmatic police auditing has increased significantly. The U.S. General Accounting Office's government auditing standards apply to all recipients of federal assistance, including states, counties, cities, and other local governmental units (Tierney, 1996). The hiring grant program, set up by Congress through the 1994 Crime Control Act, allowed more than 10,000 law enforcement agencies in all 50 states to add almost 100,000 new officers. To ensure that agencies receiving federal grants do add more officers and make good on the requirement that they continue to fund the new positions when the grants run out, the Department of Justice established an auditing program in the Monitoring Division of the Office of Community-oriented Policing Services in early 1998 (LEN, 1998).

Changes and Development in Police Auditing

Traditional auditing, with the emphasis on attestation of amounts in a financial statement as of a specific point in time, sheds no information on whether an entity's operations are economical or efficient. The approach does not permit analyses of the economy and effectiveness of police activities. Hardly any insight is provided on whether the entity has achieved its goals and objectives or could have run its programs better. Simply put, financial statement audits do not address whether there are alternative and better or cheaper methods of achieving goals (Tierney, 1996).

Over the years, there has been an increased demand for reports of government stewardship, accountability, and performance. In 1972, government auditing standards declared that audits should include not only work typically done by CPAs in auditing financial statements, but also assessment of compliance with laws and regulations, analysis of efficiency and economy of operations, and evaluation of effectiveness in achieving program objectives and results (Tierney, 1996). In the 1990s, full-time police auditors emerged in some municipalities as a result of a political compromise between the demand for creating a civilian review board and strong opposition from local police unions. They perform such functions as auditing the complaint process, monitoring police investigations, reviewing police policies, enhancing transparency, and reaching out to the community outreach (Walker, 2005). Moreover, starting in 2007, independent auditors of both private and government entities are required to assess an entity's internal controls design and implementation as part of their risk assessment procedures. Auditors need to assess whether the design of an audited organization's controls meet the control objectives or attributes outlined in the Committee of Sponsoring Organizations (COSO) guidance (Graham, 2008).

The focus of police auditing has shifted from only rendering opinions on financial statements to attesting on performance, management, compliance, controls, and operations. Many police audits today are thus concerned not only with whether police funds are handled properly and in compliance with laws and regulations, but also whether police organizations are achieving the purposes for which their programs were authorized and are doing so according to sound policies and procedures.

In general, police performance has received greater emphasis in the field of police auditing. Audits with this focus are audits of results or performance, which provide assessment on whether police have achieved goals and objectives contemplated by their parent government when it appropriated funds to the police. The performance audit, according to the U.S. General Accounting Office, includes audits designed to assess a government's economy of operations, efficiency of operations, and effectiveness of operations or program results (General Accounting Office, 1994). Each of these audits has its unique objectives, requires different approaches, demands different auditing skills, and results in different audit reporting. In the course of a performance audit, auditors may also conduct voucher audits, procedural or compliance reviews, functional audits, and other evaluations of importance to the government.

Following the changes and development in the field of police auditing, this book addresses not only audits of compliance with laws and regulations, but also audits of results achieved by the expenditure of a police department's resources. The primary focus is on performance audit, relative economy and efficiency and operational results, as well as changes that can be brought about by police auditing. Since the effects of traditional police reform efforts are inconclusive and often questioned (Brodeur 1989; Reiss 1992), performance police auditing provides another potentially viable approach that warrants the attention of both the public and the police. Whether it will lead to any significant, positive changes in police organizations and operations, however, remains to be seen, and such knowledge should only be expected after careful and systematic evaluations have been completed.

What Follows

This book provides a comprehensive view of police auditing by examining the theories, standards, procedures, applications, and evaluations of police audits. It combines a description of police audits with a discussion of theories of planned change. As a result, a model of police reform through auditing has emerged. In addition, the book integrates principles of social scientific research with standards and procedures of auditing to explicate a unique approach to enhancing the effectiveness of police auditing.

Chapter 2 specifically explores the relationship between police auditing and planned organizational change. Going beyond the single focus on auditing, this chapter describes some general issues related to changing the police and discusses police auditing as a viable approach to improving police organizations. It illustrates the structure and process of planned change and how they can be used to address the issue of efficiency and effectiveness and lead to desired changes in police management and operations. It also highlights some important concepts in the theory of planned change that police auditors should be aware of in order to obtain a more effective audit. The concepts related to the structure and process of planned change can be viewed as the theoretical foundation for police auditing.

Chapter 3 introduces essential and practical government auditing standards applicable to police auditing. These standards are essential because the police, as local, state, or federal government agencies, are required to meet them. They are practical because auditors follow them in carrying out their audit activities, and whether appropriate standards are followed determines whether the end product can be termed an audit. These standards generally include objectives to be attained by conducting an audit, measurement of audit quality, and professional judgment an auditor should exercise in planning and conducting an audit.

The fourth chapter explains procedures to be followed in police auditing. Both general and specific audit procedures related to police auditing are discussed. The general procedures include a pre-audit survey, audit planning, audit evidence gathering, audit findings, and audit reporting. Specific procedures are applied to different types of police audits such as financial statement audit, financial-related audit, compliance audit, and performance audit.

Chapter 5 discusses how police auditing is practiced in a variety of police departments and profiles some common problems targeted by police auditors. These problems are usually related to economy and efficiency of a police agency, compliance with laws and regulations concerning matters of economy and efficiency, and program results and effectiveness. The chapter provides an overview of various police audits completed in the United States and United Kingdom addressing these issues.

Chapter 6 provides a review of the Office of Independent Police Auditor (IPA), an entity established at the local government level.

Unlike traditional auditors operating in a city or parent government's accounting and/or audit division or controller's office, or in an accounting and/or auditing office within a police department, or outside the government such as a private accounting/consulting firm, the IPAs are permanent independent offices at the municipal level charged with the sole responsibility to audit the police. This chapter, after going over the triggers behind the emergence of Independent Police Auditors, examines the structure of these offices and qualifications of individuals holding the auditor positions, their basic functions and responsibilities, types of cases they handle, and how they provide solutions and/or recommendations. It also looks at some of the political and professional issues surrounding these offices.

The seventh chapter discusses the importance of evaluating police audits and their implementation, and how an audit program and its implementation should be evaluated. Two major approaches, process and outcome evaluation, are examined. Process evaluation measures how police put audit recommendations into action, and outcome evaluations measure the effects of the audit recommendations after they are implemented.

Chapter 8 presents a sample audit to illustrate the process and evaluation of a police audit. It describes the auditing process, methods used in collecting evidence, audit recommendations, police response to the recommendations, and outcomes in implementing the recommendations. Four types of recommendations are presented, including those related to police organizational structure, police operations, critical incidents and crimes, and administrative services. Data used for evaluating the outcomes in these four areas includes information on changes in organizational structure, patrol workload distribution, arrest statistics, program development, administrative enhancement, and cost savings.

Chapter 9 explores the implications of police auditing as a model of planned change. It discusses how police auditing can be integrated with several interrelated constructs in this model. These constructs include internal and external pressures, organizational disequilibrium, examination and collection of data, innovative and rational decision-making, development of solutions and alternatives, implementation of change programs, maintaining and monitoring changes, and outcome evaluation. By examining these concepts in the context of police auditing, this chapter demonstrates the importance of using them as a guide for implementing an audit program and enhancing organizational efficiency and operational effectiveness. Ultimately, whether the police are able to follow these constructs may determine whether they will be able to confront the challenges in their internal and external environment and succeed in bringing about genuine changes in their organization, management, and operations.

REFERENCES

Audit Commission for Local Authorities and the National Health Service in England and Wales. (1991). Reviewing the organization of provincial police forces. *Police Papers,* February, No. 9.

Auditing and Internal Control Division. (1983a). Uniform crime reporting systems analysis: Seven major cities. Report by Bureau of Administrative Services, Chicago Police Department.

Auditing and Internal Control Division. (1983b). Detective division reporting practices. Report by Bureau of Administrative Services, Chicago Police Department.

Bowsher, C. A. (1994). Foreword. In *Government auditing standards.* Washington, D.C.: U.S. General Accounting Office.

Brodeur, J. P. (1989). Remarks on police accountability. Paper presented at the annual meeting of the International Society of Criminology in Hamburg.

Brown, R. E., Gallagher, R. P., & Williams, M. C. (1982). *Auditing performance in government: Concepts and cases.* New York: John Wiley.

Drebin, A., & Brannon, M. (1990). Police department programs. In H. P. Hatry, J. R. Fountain, Jr., J. M. Sullivan, & L. Kremer (Eds.), *Service efforts and accomplishments reporting: Its time has come.* Norwalk, CT: Government Accounting Standards Board of the Financial Accounting Foundation.

General Accounting Office. (1994). *Government auditing standards.* Washington, D.C.: U.S. Government Printing Office.

Graham, L. (2008). *Internal controls: Guidance for private, government, and nonprofit entities.* Hoboken, NJ: John Wiley & Sons.

Law Enforcement News (LEN). (1996a). GAO audit of use-of-force practice spells good news for beleaguered ATF. April 30, 444, 5.

_____. (1996b). Damning report on LAPD training draws heated reaction from brass and Task force to look at Chicago promotions. May 15, 445, 1, 7 & 15.

_____. (1996c). Camden sends out for the cavalry in the form of NJ state troopers. January 31, 438, 1 & 9.

_____. (1997a). D.C. power: Chief given broad new authority-but stricter accountability. March 31, 464, 1 & 10.

_____. (1997b). Boston PD property control under scrutiny. November 15, 477, 5.

_____. (1997c). New faces look over cops' shoulders. April 30, 466, 6.

____. (1997d). DC chief aims to clean up homicide unit. November 30, 478, 6.

____. (1998). What becomes of COPS officers when the grants run out? DoJ wants to know. January 15, 481, 1.

Lee, R. D., Jr., & Johnson, R. W. (1983). *Public budgeting systems.* Rochville, MD: Aspen.

Mackenzie, K. D. (1986). *Organizational design: The organizational audit and analysis technology.* Norwood, NJ: Ablex.

Malan, R. M. (1988). Local government evaluation in a legislative environment. In C. G. Wye & H. P. Hatry (Eds.), *Timely, low-cost evaluation in the public sector.* San Francisco: Jossey-Bass.

Mautz, R. K., & Sharaf, H. A. (1985). *The philosophy of auditing.* Sarasota, FL: American Accounting Association.

Montgomery, R. H. (1912). *Auditing: Theory and practice.* New York: Ronald Press.

Reiss, A. J. (1992). Police organization in the twentieth century. In M. Tonry & N. Morris (Eds.), *Modern policing.* Chicago: University of Chicago Press.

Stone, A. R., & S. M. DeLuca. (1994). *Police administration.* Englewood Cliffs, NJ: Prentice-Hall.

Tierney, C. E. (1996). *Government auditing: Standards and practices.* Chicago: CCH.

Walker, S. (2005). *The new world of police accountability.* Thousand Oaks, CA: Sage.

Chapter 2

THEORETICAL MODEL

Police auditing is a process that involves planned change, which demands a systematic examination of police management and operations to discover existing and potential problems in order to improve decision-making and performance. To facilitate this change, it is desirable to develop a theoretical model of the processes that are supposed to be happening and then measure intervening variables, intermediate results, and final outcomes accordingly (Skogan, 1985). The theoretical model of police auditing is concerned with the structure and process of planned change and how they might address issues of efficiency and effectiveness and lead to desired changes. The structure outlines the interaction and interplay of the police environment, police organization, and individual officers in producing changes as well as the relationship between input and output in the audit process. The process describes the essential steps taken, procedures used, or choices made by decision-makers and auditors in audit planning and implementation. As critical factors for changing organizations, these steps, procedures, or choices are the essential ingredients for successful police auditing. Understanding the theoretical model of police auditing requires in essence an understanding of the structure and process of planned change and their application to police audits. This chapter illustrates the efficacy of this model, which lays the foundation for police auditing.

Issues in Changing the Police

As has often been recognized in police literature, it is difficult to change the police due to their quasi-military organizational structure

and strong occupational subculture. Police reforms initiated by outsiders such as citizen review boards and government-appointed commissions have been found to be ineffective in changing the police organizational culture and individual officer behaviors (Brodeur, 1989;
Reiss, 1992; Walker, 2005). Reforms initiated by the police themselves
often change the image and rhetoric but not the substance of policing.
The difficulty in changing the police, however, is not simply due to
whether the change agents are outsiders or insiders. Rather, it has more
to do with the structure and process by which the changes are introduced and implemented.

Police agencies are seldom engaged in rational planning as police
administrators rarely plan their change programs based on empirical
research (Weatheritt, 1986). Despite the fact that most medium- to
large-sized police agencies have research and development offices,
they are not responsible for or capable of developing plans or initiating planned changes (Bayley, 1994). Police evaluations also indicate
that genuine management rarely occurs in the field of policing when
compared with private business administration (Goldstein, 1990; Sheehy
Commission, 1993). As Geller (1997:2) describes, many departments
have "jumped into a program with both feet, sunk in the muck, and
then compounded the problem by failing to learn from the experience." Even when police know their traditional tactics have failed,
they still have a difficult time changing their approaches and cutting
their losses. The police face a daunting challenge: Can they bring
about a genuine, substantive change or will they engage in the rhetoric
of change only? Can they find ways to work smarter instead of hard-
er? Is there a legitimate role for research and planning in changing police organizations? Can they institutionalize an organizational change
process so they are able eventually to serve their communities economically, efficiently, and effectively?

One way to confront this challenge, perhaps, is police auditing.
Different from external citizen review boards, government-appointed
commissions, or internal police reform programs, police auditing involves rigorous research and rational decision-making. Police auditors
are usually accounting professionals with knowledge and expertise in
police administration. They investigate general police practices in order to develop policies and procedures for the purpose of changing the
organization. They are able to not only identify existing deficiencies

but also locate the root causes, and they engage in monitoring and evaluating implementation of audit recommendations. Being independent from the police, they are usually able to apply their knowledge to police programs with relatively little political interference. Being neither "pure" outsiders nor "real" insiders, they stand strategically between government-appointed commissions and reform-minded police executives. This intermediate position places them close to the reality of police work while allowing them to maintain a professional distance from the police program under review. Due to this distinctive locus in the spectrum of externally and internally initiated police reforms, police auditors hold great promise in addressing various problems confronting police organizations.

In some cities in the United States, a permanent government unit often called the office of police auditor has emerged as a new model of citizen oversight of the police. Consistent with the role of auditors, police auditors perform audits by collecting and analyzing data, finding patterned deficiencies, and recommending policy changes. As all previous police reform programs, the auditor model is not without its limitations. One of the major weaknesses is public credibility. Community leaders usually focus their energy on individual cases of police misconduct; because the auditor does not directly investigate individual complaints, they do not view this model as an effective form of oversight and thus do not lend their support to it. Another issue is the lack of political will in achieving higher police accountability in the city government. Besides an enabling ordinance that directs the auditor to review policies and procedures, a serious commitment on the part of public officials is necessary for an auditor's success (Walker, 2005).

The Structure of Planned Change

Planned change refers to a set of activities designed to change individuals, groups, and organizational structure and process (Goodman & Kurke, 1982). The potential for police auditing to create rational and significant changes lies in the employment of a theoretical model of planned change. This model is concerned with both the structure and process of planned change in the environment of police auditing. The structure of planned change delineates the structural relationship of major elements in planned change, the purposes of such change, and

the characteristics of change efforts. To understand the structural relationship in police auditing, one needs to view the theoretical model
from a broad perspective. When viewed in such a manner, the theoretical model of police auditing is analogous to an input and output
system. The input involves the audit team, police agency being audited, public officials, political constituents, and any other group that has
a legitimate interest in and contributes to the audit. The output is
about what happens as a result of the audit, which may include greater
compliance with rules and regulations in police administration, more
efficient police operations, or more rationally executed police programs. Between input and output is a transformation process, which
involves the interaction of people and technical systems in creating
outputs (Weisbord, 1991). In police auditing, the transformation process involves turning police resources into activities and then into results and outcomes.

The input and output relationship can be further examined by u-
sing two interrelated concepts, i.e., performance gap and performance
measurement. Performance gap is often the indicator of planned
change as part of the input and performance measurement indicates
whether the gap has been bridged at the time measuring the output.
Performance gap occurs when police perform below their capacity in
comparison to industry standards. Theoretically speaking, planned
change will not occur without a performance gap being identified first.
Performance gap, however, is rarely self-identified; it is more commonly exposed under environmental pressures, due to internal conflicts, or when organizational members perceive the need to change
(Warren, 1977). Progressive police administrators thus should actively
investigate the possible existence of performance gaps by staying alert
to the need for change and innovation (Klofas, Stojkovic, & Kalinich,
1990).

Performance gap may also be defined as organizational disequilibrium (Chin, 1966), resulting from such factors as employee turnover,
internal structural change, environmental conflict, and repercussions
of an agency's performance (Downs, 1967). Employee turnover often
results in the loss of experienced officers because training of new recruits takes time and cannot replace years of experience developed on
the job. Internal structural changes require that the police become
either more centralized for the purpose of higher efficiency or decen-

tralized in the name of greater effectiveness in police operations. In both cases, structural changes will create changes in personnel relationship and hierarchical order, which the organization must adapt to. Environmental conflicts affecting police organizations are usually created by strong public pressure. Pubic pressure, however, should not be viewed as a clear-cut public demand. As Williams and Wagoner (1992) pointed out, a "triad" of publics exists that can bring about three different types of changes: citizen-based change, interest group-based change, and elite-based change. These types of changes do not necessarily work separately. Rather, police changes may occur in response to a mixture of different types of public demands. Lastly, repercussions of an agency's underperformance are often the result of a routine agency activity or event (Downs, 1967). For example, advanced communications and reporting technology supplied by computer systems have created a rather clear performance gap in the police systems (Klofas et al., 1990).

While performance gap indicates problems or issues to be addressed at the point of input, performance measurement demonstrates whether the gap has been filled at the point of output. Performance measurement is concerned with program integrity, program outcome, input-output relationship, and police accountability. Since the final outcomes of a change effort may be different from what agency officials had envisioned (Sieber, 1981), conscious efforts must be maintained to keep it in place and protect its integrity once a program is up and running (Skolnick & Bayley, 1986). Appropriate methods for evaluating service delivery and programs must also be developed to measure the final outcomes (Klofas et al., 1990). The outcomes of planned changes can be evaluated according to the goals and objectives set at the outset or input stage. Without performance measures related to both inputs and outputs, it is difficult to know which elements of the management structure have actually added value (Audit Commission, 1991). Traditionally, control procedures limited accountability only to the input side of public-agency transactions—to the objects or resources allocated to an agency. This type of measurement and control of inputs hardly accounts for outputs or explains whether the expenditures resulted in a beneficial delivery of goods and services. The theory of planned change requires that a relationship be drawn between input and output. And the effort in evaluating this relationship lies at the heart of making police agencies accountable (Hudzik & Cordner, 1983).

In addition to this input-output relationship, the structure of planned change can be viewed as a bridge that links a police agency's internal programs with its environment and fills the space between the organization's today and tomorrow. Between the organization's current conditions and future prospects is a series of bridging strategies used by decision-makers (Scott, 1977). Planned change, therefore, assumes some possibility of affecting the future, or at least some effort in consciously preparing for that future (Hudzik & Cordner, 1983). This view of bridging the gap between the police and their environment, between the present and the future, is grounded in the philosophy of rationalism, a strong tradition in planning thought and theory.

The structure of the planned change model relates also to purposes and characteristics of planned change. The purposes are founded in economic thinking and decision-making theory. Economic thinking and its variants in policing have been found in appeals for quality management to reduce costs, continuing education and accreditation to reduce liability and civil law suits, and new information technologies to reduce pass-through costs and increase outputs (Manning, 1995). The planning characteristics described by Davidoff and Reiner (1962) include the achievement of ends, when planning incorporates a concept of a purposive process keyed to preferred, ordered ends; exercise of choice, as the characteristic intellectual act of planning; orientation to the future, when time is a valued and depletable resource consumed in effecting any end; action, when planning is employed to bring about results; and comprehensiveness, when the planner must detail fully the ramifications of proposals in order to allow decision-makers to choose rationally among alternative programs.

The Process of Planned Change

The idea of rationalism applies also to the process of planned change, which can be viewed as a cognitive activity aimed at producing valid and objective information for the improvement of police decision-making. This process describes functional or instrumental planning, in which planners address changes primarily as an intellectual process for efficiently adapting means to given ends and helping organizations accomplish their goals (Friedmann & Hudson, 1974). One of the traditional rational approaches is the choice theory, which suggests that planning is a process or set of procedures applied to a particular issue under consideration. Three levels of choices constitute that planning process, including the selection of ends or goals; the identification and selection of means for achieving those goals; and the effectuation, or the guidance, of action (Davidoff & Reiner, 1962). The process of planned change is further illustrated by Bayley (1994) as a strategic model consisting of several crucial elements, including collecting information about future conditions, formulating plans to meet these conditions, and estimating the costs of and the time required for implementation. Similarly, Walter and Choate (1984) characterize the approach to change as a strategic planning and management model, which includes five interrelated components: foresight, goal setting, strategic planning, operational management, and evaluation. Foresight is focused on defining long-term trends and events. The central idea for goal setting is to establish priorities for change for the organization. At the stage of strategic planning, the planner should be able to define objectives for change. Operational management is the implementation of the plan or translating the objectives established in the strategic plan into specific work programs. Evaluation examines whether the plan has been implemented as planned or whether the objectives have been met.

If the structure of planned change seems abstract, the process of planned change is concrete. It informs decision-makers on how people and technical systems interact in creating outputs (Weisbord, 1991) and how the gap between the police and their environment is actually bridged. It provides intellectual guidance to planners in their decision-making activities such as systematic information gathering, searching for solutions and alternatives, and selection of a course of action. Systematic information gathering activities serve to initiate the rational planning process, which requires that police planners gather all pertinent information without being constrained by time or other resource limitations (Klofas et al., 1990). They must survey the situation and examine the nature of the problems to ensure that systematic and comprehensive information is truly collected. To do so, they should avoid hunches and personal experiences from replacing systematic and comprehensive data collection and gather input from as many diverse sources as possible such as their constituents, the work environment, and agency members. They will also need to identify data needs, data-collection points, data collectors, and records-keeping systems.

Although undergoing this initiation process seems tedious and even unnecessary when decision-makers are concerned with an immediate managerial or operational issue, it serves to benefit the long-run health of a police organization, to which police executives should have an ongoing and substantive commitment. Similar to what Geller (1997) describes as the benefits of a learning organization, systematic information gathering allows planners to diagnose problems more accurately, pin down with supporting data what works in battling crime and disorder and in building community justice and peace, and learn about what is average and what is excellent level of performance in an industry so that standards can be articulated as the object of professional aspiration. This rational planning approach ensures that police administrators fully understand existing and potential problems that cause noncompliance, inefficiency, or ineffectiveness. These initial planning activities also help the agency officials remember the lessons of history so they can be better prepared to face a similar crisis and make better decisions (Fyfe, Greene, Walsh, Wilson, & McLaren, 1997).

Only when agency officials are committed to the long-term health of their organization will they comprehensively examine potential agency problems to determine their nature. These problems may relate to the substantive mission of the police organization, to certain fundamental agency policy and procedures, or to certain circumstantial factors. Only after problems are understood with some clarity can agency officials start to develop and ultimately implement rational solutions. In reality, however, police officials are notorious for making decisions according to personal preferences rather than sufficient planning and research. Police officials, for example, often focus on crime fighting as their major or even sole mission and ignore the vast service aspect of policing (Adams, 1971). Commitment to the agency's long-term health requires that decision-makers discover and examine the basic organizational problems that create both low productivity and low morale (March & Simon, 1967). They will then restructure accordingly their agency's goals, policies, procedures, practices, and behaviors.

Understanding the nature of an organization's problems is a prerequisite for setting goals and objectives, developing solutions and alternatives, and selecting a course of action. The rational planning process has the potential for clarifying goals and prioritizing agency objectives and enabling agency officials to develop solutions (Klofas et al., 1990). The development of solutions includes consideration of possible alternatives for the problems because these solutions must be based on an understanding of present and future constraints (Hudzik & Cordner, 1983; Scott, 1977). Development of alternatives ultimately distinguishes rational planned change from traditional police planning, making some planning experts argue that planned change should only be considered having occurred after innovative alternatives had been implemented. In the process of developing solutions and alternatives, decision-makers must be innovative and regard problems as opportunities for pursuing genuine improvement in an agency's performance. To do so, they need to set aside traditional management styles and thinking, and free themselves and their personnel from firmly-rooted organizational values that, in themselves, contain major obstacles for change (Klofas et al., 1990). They need instead to capitalize on an agency's own and others' experiences to continually hone strategies, tactics, operations, and networks of collaborators. They then must develop operational and quantifiable measures of goals and objectives and/or their alternatives, identify evaluation measures and techniques, and identify methods of analysis to be used and points at which analysis is to take place (Hudzik & Cordner, 1983).

The intellectual process of planned change should be more effective when combined with the social process of planned change. This aspect of change is concerned with organizational development, which can be defined as a series of approaches to changing an organization's climate (French, 1969). In comparison to rationalism in planning, organizational development is considered normative in planning theory. The roles of the planner and the decision-maker are less distinct, and planning is more of a social act than a cognitive one. The planner or decision-maker's role is focused primarily on developing an organization and individual members of the organization for bringing about effective changes. To do so, planners must identify aids and obstacles to change. They then should alter values, routines, and structures of a system simultaneously in an attempt to create an atmosphere in which obstacles to change can be minimized (Friedmann & Hudson, 1974). The aids and obstacles to change become the principal components of the planning environment for organizational development (Hudzik et al., 1983).

The obstacles to change include both organizational and personal sources of resistance to change. Organizational sources may involve inappropriate reward system, unwillingness to cooperate, interdepartmental rivalry, change of current balance of power between groups, prevailing organizational climate, and structural rigidity (Steers, 1977). Personal sources may include misunderstanding of purpose, mechanics, or consequences of change; failure to see the need for change; fear of loss of status, security, or power; lack of identification or involvement with change; and conflicting personal and organizational objectives (Steers, 1977). An example of personal resistance to change is the officers' fear of loss of status in community policing. Where community policing or foot patrol is being implemented, community police officers who walk the beat may be viewed by other officers as "social workers" instead of "real cops" (Trojanowicz & Carter, 1988). Geller (1997) identified some instances of personal resistance to empirical research, which include skepticism about research as ivy tower and impractical, unwillingness to cooperate with outside researchers because too often outside researchers have failed to provide feedback to assist the police, distrust of any evaluation research contending that research findings developed in another jurisdiction do not have any application at home, and reluctance to have cherished views challenged.

The extent to which police executives are able to overcome sources of resistance to change ultimately determines whether planned change will be successfully implemented (Bennis, 1966; Zaltman, Duncan, & Holbeck, 1973; Skolnick et al., 1986). Agency officials must be willing to expend the resources required to carry out change and allocate resources in line with program goals and operational priorities (Audit Commission, 1991). Because planned change and innovation of any magnitude in police organizations will invariably involve environmental concerns, communication, decision-making, job design and enrichment, personnel motivation, and power (Klofas et al., 1990), agency officials need to use a series of human relation skills to create an organizational climate conducive to change and foster communication and criticism from the ranks (Duffee, 1986; Klofas et al., 1990). Experiences in some police departments suggest that the climate for change can be created when a relatively clear mandate is given by the chief, when preparatory experiments or efforts are organized, when clear authority to implement is granted, and when rewards are linked to performance.

Major modifications may also be required in individual behaviors to overcome personal resistance to change. If organizational members are defensive and insecure, they will not be willing to venture into new roles, even if their new roles are prescribed by management (Klofas et al., 1990). Agency officials should practice organizational development techniques and programs such as survey feedback, team-building, participatory management, redefinition of personal relationships, and investment in developing individual officers to fill new roles in the process of planned change. The key group police executives should target in using these techniques and programs is police mid-management. As Kelling and Bratton (1993) suggested, police executives should create a strong vision of the business of their organization and make sure that all mid-managers share this vision and are well prepared to provide leadership in innovation. When police mid-managers are involved in the process of planning innovations, they are capable of providing instrumental leadership regardless of whether the innovations are programmatic or strategic. Alternatively, whenever police managers are kept out of planning or perceived as a resistance, they are a potentially strong source of resistance. Police chiefs have to acknowledge that mid-managers have legitimate vested self-interests that must be served if commitment to change is to be secured. When innovations threaten mid-managers' achievement records and performance indicators, it should be expected that they would be less than enthusiastic about change.

SUMMARY

Police auditing involves planned change and therefore should be guided by the theoretical model of planned change. This model depicts the structure of police organizational and operational change, describes the processes that are supposed to be happening, and guides the evaluator's effort in measuring intervening variables, intermediate results, and final outcomes of change programs. The theoretical model of planned change has strong implications for police auditing because of its role in helping the police change their usual practices, increase their efficiency, and improve their performances. Following the model may also help the police reduce the common problems encountered by traditional police reformers who often failed to see significant progress in their change efforts. Instead of blaming the quasi-military organizational structure and strong occupational subculture in police organizations, future reformers should pay more attention to the structure and process of their change efforts, which make up the theoretical model of planned change as well as police auditing.

The structure of the planned change model as applied to police auditing outlines the structural relationship of major elements in the change process, including the interaction between the environment and police, the interplay between leadership and individual members of the police organization, the link between the present and future conditions of the department, and the relationship between input and output in police auditing. The structural relationship can be further examined by looking at performance gap and performance measurement, the two concepts that indicate how an input-output relationship in police auditing is measured. The structure of the model also describes the purposes of police auditing, which include higher efficiency, better compliance with laws and regulations, and greater effectiveness in police management and operations. Furthermore, it reflects certain characteristics of planned change including a purposive process, exercise of choice, orientation to the future, action, and comprehensiveness.

The process of the model specifically delineates how resources from input are translated into police activities, and how people and technical systems interact in creating output. In bridging the gap between the police and their environment, decision-makers engage in the process of problem identification, collection of information, searching for solutions and alternatives, selection of a course of action, implementation of change plans, and evaluation of change efforts. The process of planned change is grounded in the philosophy of rationalism, which requires that planners address changes as an intellectual process of efficiently adapting means to given ends so organizations can accomplish their goals in the most cost-effective manner. To bring about changes through police auditing, decision-makers must deal with not only the intellectual but also the social aspect of planned change. In contrast to intellectual or rational process of planning, the social aspect of planning involves development of organizations and individuals for change. Creating a rational plan, therefore, is only half of the battle for planned change; the other half, which is just as critical, is to bring the plan to fruition, which involves genuine efforts in reducing both organizational and individual resistance to change.

REFERENCES

Adams, T. F. (1971). *Police patrol: Tactics and techniques.* Englewood Cliffs, NJ: PrenticeHall.

Audit Commission of Local Authorities and the National Health Service in England and Wales. (1991). Reviewing the organization of provincial police forces. *Police Papers,* February, No. 9.

Bayley, D. H. (1994). *Police for the future.* New York: Oxford University Press.

Bennis, W. (1966). Leadership in administrative behavior. In W. Bennis, K. Benne, & R. Chin (Eds.), *The planning of change.* New York: Holt, Rinehart & Winston.

Brodeur, J. P. (1989). Remarks on police accountability. Paper presented at the annual meeting of the International Society of Criminology in Hamburg.

Chin, T. (1966). The utility of system models and developmental models for practitioners. In W. Bennis, K. Benne, & R. Chin (Eds.), *The planning of change.* New York: Holt, Rinehart & Winston.

Davidoff, P., & Reiner T. A. (1962). A choice theory of planning. *Journal of the American Institute of Planners, 30,* 103–115.

Downs, A. (1967). *Inside bureaucracy.* Boston: Little, Brown.

Duffee, D. (1986). *Correctional management: Change and control in correctional organizations.* Prospect Heights, IL: Waveland Press.

French, W. L. (1969). Organizational development: Objectives, assumptions and strategies. *California Management Review, 12*(2), 23–35.

Friedmann, J., & Hudson, B. (1974). Knowledge and action: A guide to planning theory. *Journal of the American Institute of Planners, 42*(January).

Fyfe, J. J., Greene, J. R., Walsh, W. F., Wilson, O. W., & McLaren, R. C. (1997). *Police administration.* New York: McGraw-Hill.

Geller, W. A. (1997). Suppose we are really serious about police departments becoming "learning organizations"? *National Institute of Justice Journal, 234,* 2–8.

Goldstein, H. (1990). *Problem-oriented policing.* Philadelphia: Temple University Press.

Goodman, P. S., & Kurke, L. B. (1982). Studies of change in organizations: A status report. In P. S. Goodman (Ed.), *Changes in organizations: New perspectives on theory, research, and practice.* San Francisco: Jossey-Bass.

Hudzik, J. K., & Cordner, G. W. (1983). *Planning in criminal justice organizations and systems.* New York: Macmillan.

Kelling, G. L., & Bratton, W. J. (1993). Implementing community policing: The administrative problem. *Perspectives on policing: A publication of the National Institute of Justice, 17,* 1–11.

Klofas, J., Stojkovic, S., & Kalinich, D. (1990). *Criminal justice organizations: Administration and management.* Pacific Grove, CA: Brooks/Cole.

Manning, P. K. (1995). TQM and the future of policing. *Police Forum, 5*(2), 1–5.

March, J. G., & Simon, H. A. (1958). *Organizations.* New York: Wiley.

Reiss, A. J. (1992). Police organization in the twentieth century. In M. Tonry & N. Morris (Eds.), *Modern policing.* Chicago: University of Chicago Press.

Scott, W. R. (1977). Effectiveness of organizational effectiveness studies. In P. S. Goodman & J. M. Pennings (Eds.), *New perspectives on organizational effectiveness.* San Francisco: Jossey-Bass.

Sheehy Commission. (1993). Sheehy Commission report. London: HMSO.

Sieber, S. (1981). *Fatal remedies: The irony of social intervention.* New York: Plenum Press.

Skogan, W. (1985). *Evaluating neighborhood crime prevention programs.* The Hague, Netherlands: Ministry of Justice, Research and Documentation Centre.

Skolnick, J. H., & Bayley, D. H. (1986). *The new blue line: Police innovation in six American cities.* New York: Free Press.

Steers, R. M. (1977). *Organizational effectiveness: A behavioral view.* Santa Monica, CA: Goodyear.

Trojanowicz, R., & Carter, D. (1988). *The philosophy and role of community policing.* East Lansing, MI: National Neighborhood Foot Patrol Center.

Walker, S. (2005). *The new world of police accountability.* Thousand Oaks, CA: Sage.

Walter, S., & Choate, P. (1984). *Thinking strategically.* Washington, D.C.: Council of State Planning Agencies.

Warren, R. (1977). *Social change and human purpose: Toward understanding and action.* Chicago: Rand McNally.

Weatheritt, M. (1986). *Innovations in policing.* London: Croom Helm.

Weisbord, M. R. (1991). *Organizational diagnosis: A work of theory and practice.* Reading, MA: Addison-Wesley.

Williams, F. P., & Wagoner, C. P. (1992). Making the police proactive: An impossible task for improbable reasons. *Police Forum, 2*(2), 1–5.

Zaltman, G., Duncan, R., & Holbeck, J. (1973). *Innovations and organizations.* New York: Wiley.

Chapter 3

PRACTICAL STANDARDS

The theoretical model covered in the previous chapter should serve as general guidance for police auditors as they consider the practical issues surrounding an audit. The practical issues revolve around two interrelated aspects of police auditing: standards and procedures. Auditing standards are concerned with the objectives to be attained through auditing, measures of the quality of auditors' performance in auditing, and professional judgments an auditor exercises (Tierney, 1996). It is critical that auditing standards be followed because the police represent local, state, and federal government and auditors are required to meet government-stipulated standards. If inappropriate standards are followed in the course of audit work, audit practitioners and theorists generally believe that the end product cannot be termed an audit (Malan, 1997:Chap. 30). The discussion of audit standards, therefore, should precede that of audit procedures. It is important to note, however, that audit standards and procedures are two sides of the same coin. They are covered in separate chapters for better clarification and illustration of related concepts only.

Two Major Audit Approaches: Financial and Performance

A framework for standardizing audit approaches emerged in 1972, when the U.S. General Accounting Office issued the first edition of its government auditing standards. These standards set forth three elements of a "full scope" government audit: (1) financial and compliance; (2) economy and efficiency; and (3) program results or effectiveness (Stepnick, 1997: Chap. 9). The first element, the financial and compliance audit, represents the most traditional approach to government auditing. It is based on the premise that public officials entrusted with handling public resources are responsible for safeguarding the resources; ensuring that reliable data are obtained, maintained, and fairly disclosed; providing appropriate reports to those they are accountable to; and complying with applicable laws and regulations. For these purposes, governments in the United States have established a relatively elaborate system of financial and administrative controls, including the financial and compliance audits, to monitor and oversee revenues and expenditures and to report to the taxpaying public (Malan, 1997: Chap. 30).

The second and third elements, commonly termed performance audits, often cause greater concerns to police auditors. They are established to ensure that government officials not only protect the assets provided by the public, but also manage them efficiently and effectively. Police administrators, as all other public officials, are expected not only to apply public resources efficiently and economically, but also to achieve the purposes for which the resources are furnished. With these goals in mind, police managers should establish and maintain effective controls to ensure that appropriate aims and objectives are met. At a time when state and municipal governments suffer from budget gaps and fiscal cutback, performance audits force the public and government to seek better ways to make the police functions more efficient and effective. Performance audits are also based on the belief that enormous opportunities exist for increasing police efficiency and effectiveness. These types of audits, comprising of efficiency and effectiveness audits, have become a major audit approach practiced in federal agencies and is increasing in popularity in state and local governments (Malan, 1997: Chap. 30).

When the two major audit approaches, financial and performance, are combined, they form a full-scale audit program that requires a blend of financial, functional, and performance audits to allow a comprehensive examination and continuous monitoring of an activity, a program, a function, or even an entire organization. The term "audit," as used in the public sector, therefore, generally includes both financial and performance audit. Although financial and performance audits are different in their initiation, implementation, and utilization, they complement and aid each other. For example, the question on police patrols is a performance question when police managers want to know if patrol vehicles are used for things they are intended for, or for fulfilling their original purposes. The question becomes a financial one when they ask whether sufficient funds have been allocated to patrol fleet maintenance. Both financial and performance audits will note the problem but will direct a city council or police executive to different aspects of the problem. Taken together, these two types of audits provide a comprehensive understanding of the problem. More specifically, the financial audit demonstrates the existence of expenditure problems while the performance audit indicates how to correct them, which may require a change in management practice (Cox, 1992).

It is important to point out that the two audit approaches are much more different in concept than in usage. In practical terms, a financial audit often includes assessment of efficiency and effectiveness, and a performance audit may involve financial and compliance evaluation. Occasionally, the term "special-scope audit" is used to avoid the narrowing connotative effect of a financial or performance audit. Special-scope audits refer to those that address rather broad or very narrow issues that can be roughly defined as either financial or operational. These audits may involve any aspect of police activity auditors are qualified to review in terms of their knowledge, skill, and experience. They can be tailored to specific police needs, and auditors utilizing them have an excellent opportunity to develop flexible, creative audit approaches and write useful, informative audit reports (Stepnick, 1997: Chap. 9).

This broadly accepted program of auditing for both financial statements and police performance, however, is neither formally planned nor centrally mandated. Each audit has its own objectives and requires auditors and reviewers with differing skills because each audit is directed toward different questions about an entity's relative financial position, economy, efficiency, and effectiveness. Due to the particular concern of each audit, financial and performance audits can be further classified, conceptually, into five different types of audits, namely, financial statement audit, financial-related audit, compliance audit, efficiency audit, and effectiveness audit. Compliance audit, although frequently defined as a separate audit, is more commonly used as a part of any one of the other four audits. A case that illustrates the overlapping of compliance audit with financial statement audit is the Passage of the Single Audit Act of 1984. Many auditors believe that this act marked the emergence of an improved system for auditing non-federal entities such as state and local police departments that receive federal funds. Under the single audit system, a recipient agency's internal controls and its compliance with laws and regulations pertaining to federal awards are audited in conjunction with the basic audit of its financial statements rather than as separate special audits. Under the Single Audit Act Amendments of 1996, single audit requirements apply only when the agency expends total federal awards of $300,000 or more in a fiscal year. In addition, efficiency audit is usually conducted together with effectiveness audit and is, therefore, often discussed under the term "performance audit."

In the following sections of this chapter, the general standards that apply to most audits are introduced first, and then a brief discussion of the objectives and standards of financial statement audit, financial-related audit, and compliance audit is provided. Due to the particular concern of police agencies for performance audits and the focus of this book on changing the police through auditing, the last section of this chapter is devoted to a detailed discussion of the objectives, definition, and standards of performance audits.

General Government Auditing Standards

The fundamental purpose of government auditing standards is to ensure "full accountability" of governments and their management. The U.S. General Accounting Office (GAO) publishes these standards, often referred to as the "yellow book," which provide guidance for both financial audits and performance audits of government funds, organizations, programs, activities, and functions. Federal laws have extended the scope of the government auditing standards to audits of almost any entity receiving federal financial assistance.

According to the Budget and Accounting Procedures Acts of 1916 and 1950, these standards apply to all matters relating to the receipt, disbursement, and application of public funds, whether made by a federal governmental department or agency, or state or local governmental entity, or federal contractor, grantee, or other organization who receive federal financial assistance. Auditing regulations imposed by other governments do not supersede the generally accepted professional and government auditing standards. The auditor has the responsibility to comply with all appropriate and applicable audit requirements, e.g., auditing criteria developed by the American Institute of Certified Public Accountants (AICPA), General Accounting Office (GAO), Federal Office of Management and Budget (OMB), Federal Inspectors General, and state and local governments (Tierney, 1996).

The American Institute of Certified Public Accountants (AICPA) originally promulgated the generally accepted auditing standards in the form of Statements on Auditing Standards (SASs). The U.S. General Accounting Office (GAO) generally accepts the SASs as applicable government auditing standards unless the GAO officially rejects them through formal announcements. The AICPA's generally accepted auditing standards are primarily directed toward dictating the necessary minimum performance by an auditor to support the rendering of an opinion on financial statements. However, many AICPA standards developed for financial audits are directly related to performance because the financial audits' scope includes an evaluation of efficiency and effectiveness (U.S. Comptroller General, 1994; The Institute of Internal Auditors, 1987).

The general government auditing standards for both financial and performance audits are concerned with the staff assigned to conduct the audit, independence of audit organization and individual auditors, and professional care (AICPA, 1994). The staff assigned to conduct the audit should collectively possess adequate technical training and professional proficiency for the tasks required. In all matters relating to the audit work, the audit organization and the individual auditors, whether government or public, should be free from personal and external impairments to independence. Because police auditors within municipal governments are established either by ordinance or created under terms of consent decrees or engaged under contracts, the degree of their political independence may vary from city to city due to differences in their authority and structure (Walker, 2005). Regardless, all police auditors should be organizationally independent and maintain an independent attitude and appearance. And due professional care must be exercised in the performance of an audit and preparation of an audit report.

According to Public Company Accounting Oversight Board (PCAOB) Standards (AS2, Section 47), the auditor should obtain an understanding of the design of specific controls by making inquiries of appropriate management, supervisory, and staff personnel; inspecting company documents; observing the application of specific controls; and tracing transactions through the information system relevant to financial reporting (Switzer, 2007). Audit documentation must also be prepared according to the standards of the PCAOB in sufficient detail to provide a clear understanding of the engagement's purpose, source, and conclusions reached. The documentation "should be appropriately organized to provide a clear link to the significant findings or issues" (Switzer, 2007:205).

Each audit organization conducting audits in accordance with these standards should have an appropriate internal quality control system in place and undergo an external quality control review. The responsibility lies with the audit organization for ensuring that the audit is done in accordance with these standards and that the audit coverage is broad enough to fulfill the reasonable needs of audit report users. Auditors should assist public officials and others in understanding the auditors' responsibilities under generally accepted government auditing standards (GAGAS) and audit coverage required by laws and regulations. This comprehensive nature of auditing highlights the importance of having a clear understanding of audit objectives, scope of work to be conducted, and reporting requirements for auditors (GAO, 1994).

The General Accounting Office (1994) has also stipulated general standards for audit planning and audit reporting. These are usually the beginning and end of an audit engagement. Standard audit plans usually contain information about legal and/or other authority for an audit, proposed audit objectives, scope and methodologies, staff responsibilities, assignments, and audit programs. In planning an audit, auditors should consider significance and needs of potential users for the audit report, legal and regulatory requirements, and management controls. They should obtain an understanding of the programs to be audited, identify criteria needed for evaluating related matters, and research potential sources of audit evidence. In addition, they should identify significant findings and recommendations from previous audits that may affect the current audit, see if corrective action has been taken, and consider whether the work of other auditors and experts should be used to satisfy some of the current audit objectives. Finally, they should provide sufficient staff and other resources to do the audit and prepare a written audit plan.

A standard audit report should state that the audit was made in accordance with generally accepted government auditing standards (GAGAS) and communicate certain information related to the conduct and reporting of the audit, including the engagement's objectives, scope, auditor's overall opinion and conclusions, recommendations, and action plans (Switzer, 2007). A written audit report is to be submitted by the audit organization to appropriate officials of the audited agency and of organizations requiring or arranging for the audit, including external funding organizations, unless legal restrictions prevent the audit agency from doing so. Copies of the report should also be sent to other officials who have legal oversight authority or who may be responsible for acting on audit findings and recommendations and to others authorized to receive such reports. Unless restricted by law or regulation, copies should be made available for public inspection as well.

Financial Statement Audit Standards

The objective of financial statement audits is to provide reasonable assurance that the financial statements fairly present the financial position, results of operations, and cash flows of a police department in a manner consistent from one fiscal period to the next. The audit standards for financial statement audits include generally accepted government auditing standards (GAGAS) of the U.S. GAO and the generally accepted auditing standards (GAAS) and statements on auditing standards (SASs) of the AICPA. The government auditing standards incorporate existing and any new AICPA standards relevant to financial statement audits unless the GAO specifically excludes these standards by formal announcement. These incorporated standards are more popularly referred to as the "attestation standards," which are an extension of the AICPA's generally accepted auditing standards (AICPA, 1994).

Financial statement audit standards are concerned with qualifications of the auditing practitioners, conditions under which an engagement shall be performed, independence of the auditors, and professional care in the performance of the engagement. A practitioner or practitioners having adequate technical training and proficiency in the attested police function and having adequate knowledge in the subject matter of the assertion shall perform the engagement. The practitioner shall perform an engagement only if he or she has reason to believe that the assertion is capable of evaluation against reasonable criteria and the assertion is capable of reasonably consistent estimation or measurement using such criteria. These criteria should either have been established by a recognized body or be stated in the presentation of the assertion in a sufficiently clear and comprehensive manner for a knowledgeable reader to understand. In all matters relating to the engagement, the practitioner or practitioners shall maintain independence in mental attitude and exercise due professional care (AICPA, 1994).

The audit scope for financial statement audits is prescribed and generally accepted. The audit work within the scope should be adequately planned and auditing assistants, if any, should be properly supervised. Auditors should obtain sufficient evidence to provide a reasonable basis for the conclusion they express in a report. Audit reports are also prescribed, including uniform, standard form opinion and content (Tierney, 1996). A report should either describe the scope of the auditors' testing of police compliance with laws and regulations and internal controls and present the results of those tests or refer to separate reports containing that information.

Although auditors routinely conduct tests of internal controls, internal controls are the responsibility of management, which involve designing and implementing systems and procedures for the prevention and detection of financial fraud. A concept of a fraud triangle has been refined as motivation, opportunity, and rationalization (AICPA, 2002; Graham, 2008). Management is thus responsible also for creating a culture of honesty and ethics and a positive working environment (Graham, 2008). The awareness of fraud risk and abuse should be raised to motivate better controls design and monitoring. Better internal controls, more auditor attention to controls design, and more fraud awareness should reduce frauds over time (Graham, 2008).

Financial-Related Audit Standards

Financial-related audits are similar to financial statement audits in terms of objectives and standards. They determine whether financial information is presented in accordance with established or stated criteria, whether an audited agency has adhered to specific financial compliance requirements, and whether the audited agency's internal control structure over financial reporting and asset safeguarding is suitably designed and implemented to achieve the control objectives. Financial-related audits are, however, different from financial statement audits in terms of audit scope and audit report (Tierney, 1996). As far as the police are concerned, a financial-related audit is an audit reporting on selected programs or units of their organization. Uniquely designed for each situation, a financial-related audit can be as diverse as the number of audits made. Generally it has an audit scope other than or less than a comprehensive annual financial report or general-purpose financial statements of a police agency or a defined component of a police agency. Financial-related audits usually include examining the adequacy of financial systems in support of operational decisions. Financial-related auditors conduct audits of controls, expenditures, and compliance of various functional activities or organizations, such as personnel and payroll, procurement, and grants management. They perform program audits of agency management and the constituent program contractors or grantees.

The financial-related audit of compliance of individual contracts or grants or cooperative agreements requires that auditors examine the terms and conditions of an agreement and identify services or performance to be rendered and then assess the actual status of performance. The auditors compare the approved financial budget and planned expenditure rates to amounts incurred, recorded in the accounting records, and reported and billed to the sponsoring organization. They test the costs incurred and charged to the budget categories of the agreement for compliance with terms and conditions and any allowable or unallowable or matching cost prescriptions imposed by the awarding organization. They also verify that amounts due are properly billed, received, recorded, and deposited and that ending receivables and liabilities reflect the agreement status. They test close-out procedures and practices to assess the propriety of settlement in compliance with the agreement terms and conditions; examine the reasonableness, allowableness, and allocation of indirect or overhead costs charged to the agreement activities. They confirm, with the awarding organization, the status of the agreement; review and confirm that assets and other property furnished by the awarding organization are appropriately accounted for, adequately controlled, and properly reported (GAO, 1994).

Auditors also perform post-audits of police expenditures, audits of end-of-period obligations, encumbrances, and unexpected appropriation balances. They examine and recommend improvement of alternative internal control policies and procedures. Certain aspects of any of these and other financial-related audits that could be added to the list parallel parts of the audits for economy, efficiency, and effectiveness, i.e., performance-type audits. Consequently, financial-related audit report is narrative, reporting on results and findings in relation to unique audit objectives and scope (Tierney, 1996).

Compliance Audit Standards

As mentioned earlier, compliance audit can rarely stand on its own as an independent audit type; it is described here as a separate audit mainly for conceptual clarification purposes. Compliance audit is conducted to assess police compliance with laws, regulations, rules, and management assertions. The word faithfulness is often used to describe the nature of this audit approach due to its focus on testing a police agency's faithfulness to laws and regulations. To audit police compliance with laws and regulations, auditors need to understand the control measures police use for ensuring compliance. According to AICPA (1986), to obtain an understanding of the controls for ensuring compliance, auditors should inquire the office of auditor or other oversight organization about laws and regulations applicable to police agencies within their jurisdiction and review all available information about compliance requirements. They should consider knowledge of such laws and regulations obtained from prior years' audits and discuss the laws and regulations with the agency's chief financial officer. They should also obtain written representation from police management regarding the completeness of management's identification of laws, regulations, rules, and procedures. Only after obtaining a good understanding of the controls can auditors start testing the control procedures to determine whether they have been fully implemented. Federal laws require that auditors test transactions for each major federal assistance program. Auditors, therefore, need to identify and review relevant portions of any directly related police agreements such as those contained in contracts and grants.

Generally accepted auditing standards require that compliance auditors plan and audit in a manner that allows material errors, irregularities, and instances of noncompliance to have a reasonable likelihood of being detected. Under these standards, the dollar amount is the key criterion for materiality. But, government auditing standards have also established that auditors consider certain other qualitative and quantitative issues such as the cumulative effect and impact of numerous immaterial items. AICPA (1994), in its SAS on compliance audit considerations, requires that auditors consider the effect of identified instances of noncompliance on each federal program and, additionally, the effect of identified instances of noncompliance on the financial statements undergoing audit. Auditors should examine whether any instances of noncompliance identified in the audit have resulted in questioned costs, and whether the questioned costs are material to the police program. To make conclusions relating to effect, the AICPA requires that auditors consider the frequency of noncompliance identified in the audit and the adequacy of a primary recipient's system for monitoring subrecipients. In presenting the results of compliance audits, auditors should report irregularities, illegal acts, other material noncompliance, and reportable conditions in police internal controls. In some circumstances, auditors should report irregularities and illegal acts directly to parties external to the audited agency. If certain information is prohibited from general disclosure, the audit report should state the nature of the information omitted and the requirement that makes the omission necessary.

Performance Audit Standards

Responsible police auditors must consider whether operations of police programs are economical and efficient, and whether the programs have achieved the purposes for which they were established. Such considerations ensure that police be able to identify programs or functions with low efficiency, no longer serving a purpose, or whose objectives are no longer attainable (Drucker, 1973), and take appropriate actions to address the problems. The government auditing standards are provided for efficiency and effectiveness auditing. Efficiency and effectiveness audit is more popularly termed performance audit and less known as operational audit or management audit. It can be conducted as a separate audit or used as a supplement to other government audits in financial, compliance, and contract areas (Malan, 1997: Chap. 30). Having evolved since the mid- to late 1960s, performance audits have become a regular part of audit programs of independent government audit organizations and internal auditors at the federal, state, and local levels (Stepnick, 1997: Chap. 9).

Since the purpose of a performance audit is to make a police program, function, or activity more efficient and effective in utilizing its
resources, a performance audit is aimed at improving current practices. As Greenwood (1967) stated, the traditional financial audit asks
whether it was done right; the performance audit asks how police can
change their practices to make them better. The traditional governmental auditing standards are founded in the premise that governmental accountability requires the identification of what public funds
are spent; the performance auditing standards evaluate the manner
and effectiveness of the expenditures. Unlike the traditional audit that
operates from a set of well-defined and known operating premises, the
performance audit presumes that each organizational setting is in
some way unique. As Cox (1992) indicated, the auditing strategy or focus that works in one police department at one time may not work in
another agency at another time. Under different circumstances and at
different times, a performance audit may evaluate effectiveness in controlling, utilizing, and directing human resources of an organization. It
may explore change in the structure of an organization by determining how many operating divisions are necessary, or whether the police
should centralize or decentralize functions such as investigations,
administrative records, and enforcement. It may assess the need to
increase productivity when certain crimes such as breaking and enter-
ing or auto theft are on the increase; the need for better and more
effective communications within the ranks; the need to improve morale among patrol officers and the police force in general; or the need
to reduce interpersonal and organizational conflict and improve management styles.

GAO (1994) defines a performance audit as an objective, systematic, and independent examination of the performance of a government organization, program, activity, or function to provide useful
information for improving public accountability and facilitating decision-making by parties with responsibility to oversee or initiate corrective action. The identified objectives or purposes of a performance
audit include assessing performance, identifying opportunities for improvement, and developing recommendations for improvement (AICPA,
1982). Since performance auditing is the only audit method for independently identifying, documenting, and assessing unsatisfactory performance, the independence, objectivity, depth, and breadth are

essential factors when assessing the adequacy of performance audits (Tierney, 1996).

Performance audits encompass two general types: economy and efficiency audits and program audits (GAO, 1994). Economy and efficiency audits are directed at assessing whether an organization might operate less expensively and better. The audit standards for performance audits of economy and efficiency include determinations of whether the entity is acquiring, protecting, and using its resources economically and efficiently; the causes of inefficiencies and uneconomical practices; and whether the entity has complied with laws and regulations on matters of economy and efficiency. Program audits are directed at assessing whether an entity is achieving or performing in the manner intended when a legislature or parent government provided funding for a program as well as its operations. The auditing standards for performance audit of programs include determinations of the extent to which desired results or benefits established by the legislature or other authorizing bodies are being achieved; the effectiveness of organizations, programs, activities, or functions; and whether an entity has complied with significant laws and regulations applicable to its programs. As Tierney (1996) indicated, however, the distinction between these two types of performance audits might be clearer in literature than in practice because both economy and efficiency audits and program audits are generally included in performance audits.

The government auditing standards for performance audits cover general, fieldwork, and reporting standards (GAO, 1994). The general standards are essentially the same as those for financial statement and financial-related audits. A performance audit team must be concerned with its collective professional proficiency to undertake a performance audit completely. Each individual member of the team need not him- or herself possess all of the requisite skills. Staffs involved in planning and conducting performance audits in the governmental environment should, individually or collectively, possess basic knowledge of accounting and auditing theory and procedures and the education, ability, and experience to apply such knowledge to the type of audit activities implicit in the desired performance audit. They should also have knowledge of governmental organizations and their operating programs, activities, and functions, which are usually acquired by education, experience, or study. They should possess technical skills appropriate for performing the task needed to complete the desired performance audit. After all, audit team members need a diversity of academic and technical backgrounds to examine the function areas under audit. This may require a team of persons skilled in finance, computer science, statistics, quantitative methods, law, criminal justice, as well as accounting and auditing. It is also desirable for the team to have persons knowledgeable of, or experienced in the specific program or activity to be audited. This would require recruitment of individuals with prior knowledge of or expertise in the type of police departments to be audited.

The government auditing standards require that as a minimum compliance be tested for certain legislations for performance audits. Audits of efficiency and economy require that tests be made of laws and regulations that could significantly affect acquisition, protection, and use of government resources and quantity, timeliness, and cost of products and services produced or delivered. Audits of program results require that laws and regulations pertaining to purposes of the program, manner of program delivery or operations, and population to be served or need to be addressed be examined.

Management controls is a critical area when testing compliance. Performance audit standards define management controls as including plan of organization, methods, and procedures adopted by management to ensure that its goals and objectives are met; processes for planning, organizing, directing, and controlling program operations; systems for measuring, reporting, and monitoring program performance; and policies and procedures implemented to ensure data is valid, reliable, and fairly disclosed. The controls include measures management take to ensure resource use is consistent with laws and regulations; and resources are safeguarded against waste, loss, and misuse (GAO, 1994). The absence of controls or gaps in controls design, regardless of conformance to legislation or regulation, is a reportable finding. If controls are lacking or unable to meet the control objectives, auditors will provide a communication to management and those charged with governance on the significant deficiencies and material weaknesses identified (AICPA, 1995; Graham, 2008).

Police management is ultimately responsible for establishing controls over operations and ensuring compliance with these controls. The five components of the controls framework include an organization's control environment, risk assessment, control activities, information and communication, and monitoring (Graham, 2008). In order to meet the control objectives, entities must be able to "describe the processes, procedures, and controls in place so they can be compared to the benchmark control objectives or attributes" (Graham, 2008: 110). If a material weakness exists in any COSO component or an aggregation of deficiencies leads to such a consideration, a "conclusion that internal controls are ineffective will arise" (Graham, 2008:159).

In addition to the general standards, GAO (1994) has prescribed performance audit standards with respect to fieldwork and reporting. For fieldwork, first, audit work is to be planned adequately and auditors must prepare a written plan.. It is required that audit plans contain legal and/or other authority for the audit, audit objectives, scope and methodologies, staff responsibilities, assignments, and audit programs. Second, sufficient staff and other resources are to be provided to perform the audit, and staff is to be properly supervised. Third, auditors must consider legal and regulatory requirements. When laws, regulations, and other compliance requirements are significant to audit objectives, auditors must design the audit in such a way that provides reasonable assurances about compliance with them. Fourth, auditors should obtain an understanding of the police programs to be audited, identify criteria for evaluating matters subject to auditing, and familiarize themselves with management controls that are relevant to the audit. When management controls are significant to audit objectives, auditors must gather sufficient evidence to support their judgments on the controls. Fifth, sufficient, competent, and relevant evidence is to be collected to afford a reasonable basis for auditors' findings and conclusions.

Auditors are not usually required, and may not be able to, express an overall opinion on the relative economy, efficiency, or effectiveness of a police agency subject to a performance audit. Alternatively, auditors are expected to report, in narrative forms, findings, conclusions, and recommendations arising from the performance audit (Tierney, 1996). In audit reporting, auditors should consider significance and needs of potential users of the report, identify potential sources of data that could be used as evidence, and consider the validity and reliability of the data. They should also consider whether the work of other auditors and experts can be used to satisfy some of the audit objectives, and identify significant findings and recommendations from previous audits to see if previous findings could affect the current audit objectives and if corrective actions in response to previous recommendations have been taken. A record of the auditors' work is to be retained in the form of working papers, which should contain sufficient information to allow an experienced auditor with no previous connection with the audit to ascertain the evidence that supports the auditors' significant conclusions and judgments (GAO, 1994).

There are five government auditing standards for reporting performance audits. First, auditors should prepare written audit reports communicating the results of each audit. Second, auditors should appropriately issue the reports to make the information available for timely use by management, legislative officials, and other interested parties. Third, auditors should report the audit objectives and audit scope and methodology. Fourth, the report should be complete, accurate, objective, and convincing, and as clear and concise as the subject matter permits. Fifth, written reports are be submitted by the audit organization to appropriate officials both internal and external to the audited agency.

SUMMARY

The term "audit" as known in the field of policing includes both financial and performance audits. These two audit types, when combined, form the full-scope audit covered in the government auditing standards. They are not intended, however, to apply to every audit of a police department because not all audits require or are suited to the application of a full-scope audit. The two audit types can be further broken down into five different audits that demand the attention of police administrators. These are financial statement, financial-related, compliance, efficiency, and effectiveness audits. Based upon the premise that public officials entrusted with handling public resources are responsible for safeguarding those resources, these audits are instituted to ensure that police administrators apply their resources economically, faithfully, efficiently, and effectively. To do so, they must comply with applicable laws and regulations; establish and maintain effective controls to achieve the purposes for which the resources are furnished;

ensure that appropriate goals and objectives are met; ensure that reliable data are obtained, maintained, and fairly disclosed; and provide appropriate reports to those to whom they are accountable.

Government auditing standards are concerned with the objectives to be attained through auditing, measure of the quality of auditors' performance, and professional judgments auditors exercise. The standards provide guidance in various areas of auditing, including assignment of audit staff, independence of audit organizations and individual auditors, and professional care in planning, performing, and reporting audits of police funds, programs, activities, and functions. The auditors are responsible for complying with all appropriate and applicable audit requirements.

Financial audits include financial statement, financial-related, and compliance audits. The objective of financial statement audits is to provide reasonable assurance that the financial statements fairly represent the financial position, results of operations, and cash flows of a police agency according to the generally accepted auditing standards. Financial-related audits determine whether financial information is presented in accordance with established criteria and whether the audited agency has adhered to specific financial compliance requirements; or whether the agency's internal control structure is suitably designed and implemented to achieve the control objectives. Financial statement audits and financial-related audits are different in terms of audit standards, audit scope, and audit report. While financial statement audit standards, scope, and report are prescribed and generally accepted, financial-related audits are audits of selected parts of a police agency, are uniquely designed for each individual audit, and are reports on findings in relation to unique audit objectives and scope. The compliance audit can be part of any other audit type including both financial and performance audits. Its objective is to assess compliance with laws, regulations, rules, and management assertions. Compliance auditors are required to plan and audit in a manner that causes material errors, irregularities, and instances of noncompliance to have a reasonable likelihood of being detected. They must obtain an understanding of management controls and test the controls to confirm implementation.

A performance audit is an objective, systematic, and independent examination of the performance of a police organization, program, activity, or function for the purpose of providing useful information for improving accountability and facilitating decision-making. Its objectives are to assess performance, identify opportunities for improvement, and develop recommendations for improvement. There are two general types of performance audits: economy and efficiency audits and program audits. Economy and efficiency auditors assess whether the operations of police programs are economical and efficient. Program auditors examine whether a police organization has achieved the purposes for which its programs were established or is performing in a manner intended by the legislature or other authority when funding for the programs was authorized. The general government auditing standards for police performance audits are the same as those for financial audits. Additional auditing standards, however, have been prescribed with respect to fieldwork and reporting for performance audits.

REFERENCES

AICPA. (1982). *Operational audit engagements.* New York: American Institute of Certified Public Accounts.

AICPA. (1986). *Audit and accounting guide: Audits of state and local governmental units.* New York: American Institute of Certified Public Accountants.

AICPA. (1994). *Audit and accounting guide: Audits of state and local governmental units.* New York: American Institute of Certified Public Accountants.

AICPA. (1995). *Statements on auditing standards.* No. 109, Understanding the entity and its environment and assessing the risks of material misstatement and No. 112, Communicating internal control matters identified in an audit. New York: American Institute of Certified Public Accountants.

AICPA. (2002). *Statements on auditing standards.* No. 99, Consideration of fraud in a financial statement audit. New York: American Institute of Certified Public Accountants.

Cox, R. W. (1992). Managerial concepts of control of the organization: The management audit. In H. W. More & P. C. Unsinger (Eds.), *Managerial control of the police: Internal affairs and audits.* Springfield, IL: Charles C Thomas.

Drucker, P. F. (1973). *Management: Tasks, responsibilities, practices.* New York: Harper & Row.

General Accounting Office (GAO). (1994). *Government auditing standards.* Washington, D.C.: U.S. Government Printing Office.

Graham, L. (2008). *Internal controls: Guidance for private, government, and nonprofit entities.* Hoboken, NJ: John Wiley & Sons.

Greenwood, W. T. (1967). *Business policy: A management approach.* New York: Macmillan.

Institute of Internal Auditors. (1987). *Standards for the professional practice of internal auditing.* Altamonte Springs, FL: The Institute of Internal Auditors.

Malan, R. M. (1997). Efficiency and effectiveness audits. In M. A. Dittenhofer & E. W. Stepnick (Eds.), *Applying government auditing standards.* New York: Matthew Bender & Co.

Stepnick, E. W. (1997). Special government audits. In M. A. Dittenhofer & E. W. Stepnick (Eds.), *Applying government auditing standards.* New York: Matthew Bender & Co.

Switzer, S. (2007). *Internal audit reports post Sarbanes-Oxley: A guide to process-driven reporting.* Hoboken, NJ: John Wiley & Sons.

Tierney, C. E. (1996). *Government auditing: Standards and practices.* Chicago: CCH Inc.

U.S. Comptroller General. (1994). *Government auditing standards: 1994 Revision.* Washington, D.C.: U.S. Government Printing Office.

Walker, S. (2005). *The new world of police accountability.* Thousand Oaks, CA: Sage.

Chapter 4

PRACTICAL PROCEDURES

Audit procedures are concerned about activities auditors perform during an audit engagement. They involve specific steps auditors take in planning, implementing, and completing an audit. Both general and specific government audit procedures have been applied to police auditing. This chapter first describes the general procedures required in police auditing. Specific procedures applicable to three types of police audits, i.e., financial statement, financial-related, and performance audits, are then discussed separately. Due to the particular concern of police agencies with program economy, efficiency, and effectiveness, performance audit procedures are covered more extensively.

General Police Audit Procedures

Audits are performed usually by either an internal audit office within a municipal government or an outside accounting and auditing firm. Where an internal office is not available, the first step for the police or a municipal government is to enter a contract for audit services. When contracting for audit services, it is important for the police to follow sound procurement procedures, including contract award and approval procedures and monitoring of contract performance. They must also make sure that objectives and scope of an audit are clear. Although cost is usually a concern in deciding which audit organization or auditors to hire, other factors might be more important in making a final selection, including responsiveness of the auditors to police request for proposal, experience of the auditors, availability of the audit staff with professional qualifications and technical abilities, and results of the auditors' external quality control reviews (GAO, 1994).

For auditors, only assignments within the scope of their professional expertise should be undertaken (Woolf & Hindson, 2011). They must adhere to the principles of independence, objectivity and integrity. Where "material doubt" exists, they must avoid potential conflict by declining the assignment (Woolf & Hindson, 2011:277). Throughout the audit process, they must guard against undue influence from management in order to produce a proper and strong audit. They "should not allow budgetary constraints to restrict the scope of audit work that is necessary" although small audit agencies "must remain alert to the risk that an audit assignment may grow too large" for their resources (Woolf & Hindson, 2011:90-91).

Once the task for auditing is at hand, auditors, whether internal or external, should begin audit planning activities according to appropriate time frames established by the government or stipulated in the contract. The audit planning should start with several ideals in mind in order to achieve "the highest levels of performance" (Pickett, 2006: 231), including promoting appropriate ethics and values, ensuring effective performance management and accountability, communicating effectively risk and control information, and coordinating effectively activities of auditors and management (Pickett, 2006). Auditors need also to incorporate in the planning process the expectations and requirements of political leaders and chiefs of police in charge of the audited organization, including their statutory responsibilities for protecting the welfare of the organization, ensuring compliance with relevant laws and regulations, delivering strategies that promote the achievement of organizational objectives, and employing a system of controls that guard against the risks of failures. The audit plan should "be derived from a big-picture thinking where each individual piece of audit work contributes to the growth of good governance, effective risk management, and better internal controls" (Pickett, 2006:258).

Depending on the issues to be addressed, auditors determine what information–financial, performance, management, and operational data–they should collect. They must gather, study, analyze, and conclude upon the information. They cannot simply assume that "management, by virtue of its proximate involvement with the accounting function, exerts effective supervisory controls" (Woolf & Hindson, 2011:90). They "must give proper consideration to the validity and plausibility of representations made by management and must verify such representations to independent third party documentation" (Woolf & Hindson, 2011:91). Frequently, sufficient or directly relevant documentation does not exist. In this situation, auditors must first establish an audit database or system; then collect, compile, and organize the database; and finally report appropriate information.

As a crucial part of the data collection process, audit fieldwork must be undertaken by auditors with sufficient experience in identifying anomalies in relevant activities and records. Auditors should remember that even the most basic checks can sometimes lead to evidence of wrongdoing. Suspicious activities and documentations should always be investigated until resolved (Woolf & Hindson, 2011). In addition, auditors should form their own opinions wherever independent assessment is required. They must not allow their standards to lapse in the face of management pressure. They must not "sign off until the requirement for evidence is satisfied" (Woolf & Hindson, 2011:145), keeping in mind that they lend credibility to financial and performance audit statements by the mere association of their names with those statements.

The auditing process itself usually consists of five interrelated steps (Malan, 1997). First, auditors perform a pre-audit survey, which involves collection of preliminary and background information related to the audit, to familiarize themselves with the audited agency, program, activity, or function. Second, auditors plan the audit to save time and ensure that appropriate audit objectives will be achieved. Third, they gather sufficient and relevant evidence in order to conduct a competent analysis of the audited program or function. Fourth, they develop findings from the evidence and make specific recommendations. Lastly, they prepare and write the audit report.

Financial Statement Audit Procedures

The police audit procedures for financial statement audits are mandated by the generally accepted government auditing standards (GAGAS) of U.S. General Accounting Office (GAO) and generally accepted auditing standards of AICPA. They include planning and designing the audit, conducting substantive tests, and meeting reporting requirements. In order to adequately plan the audit and determine the nature, timing, and extent of tests to be performed, auditors should obtain a sufficient understanding of the internal control structure of the police agency. This usually means that auditors are required to perform some preliminary audit work in order to understand controls and judgmental conclusions regarding assessment of control risk (Tierney, 1996). The planning and designing phase of the audit also requires that auditors design the audit in such a manner that it provides reasonable assurance of detecting material misstatements resulting from noncompliance with provisions of police contracts or grant agreements that have a direct and material effect on the determination of financial statement amounts. If specific information comes to the auditors' attention that provides evidence concerning the existence of possible noncompliance that could have a material indirect effect on the financial statement, the auditors must apply audit procedures specifically directed to ascertaining whether that noncompliance has occurred (GAO, 1994).

Substantive tests for financial statement audits are the detailed tests performed of classes of transactions and account balances and analytical review procedures. Tests of transactions are an examination of relevant support documentation to verify the authenticity of entries appearing in the formal accounting system of an entity. Tests of account balances are an examination of details of accounts to test for monetary correctness and other characteristics of general and other ledger balances that appear in the general purpose financial statements. Analytic review procedures are tests made to assess the overall reasonableness of controls, transactions, and account balances utilizing analyses, ratios, comparisons, averages, exception reporting, and other techniques to identify unusual and material variances (Tierney, 1996).

Substantive audit tests are accomplished through the performance of one, but more commonly two or more, of audit procedures to obtain evidence to support the various financial statement assertions. These procedures, according to Tierney (1996), include physical examination and observation or witnessing of police activities by auditors; obtaining and examining documents produced internally and externally for the police; confirmation of data with sources external to the police; scanning of records for unusual amounts, performed either manually or in conjunction with computerized audit tools; inquiries by auditors of senior police executives, mid-level police managers, and operating personnel; reperformance, rechecking, reconciling, recalculating of balances, dollar extensions, unit values, etc., by auditors; vouching amounts recorded in the accounts back to supporting documentation and tracking information recorded in supporting documentation to amounts shown in the account balances; and analytic procedures involving the use of comparisons, ratios, variance, and other analytical techniques to identify significant deviations or to corroborate information in the accounts, funds, and fund-type balances.

The financial audit report shall identify the assertion being reported on, state the character of the engagement, and provide auditors' conclusions on whether the assertion is presented in conformity with the established and/or stated criteria. For instance, the report shall state whether the police financial statements are presented in accordance with generally accepted accounting principles and identify those circumstances in which such principles have not been consistently observed in the current period in relation to the preceding period. All of auditors' significant reservations about the engagement to evaluate an assertion prepared in conformity with agreed-upon criteria or an engagement to apply agreed-upon procedures should contain a statement limiting its use to the parties who have agreed upon such criteria or procedures. In all cases where an auditor's name is associated with financial statements, the report should contain a clear-cut indication of the character of the auditor's work, if any, and the degree of responsibility the auditor is taking. Informative disclosures in the financial statements are to be regarded as reasonably adequate unless otherwise stated in the report (AICPA, 1994).

The report shall contain either an expression of an opinion regarding the financial statements, taken as a whole, or an assertion to the effect that an opinion cannot be rendered. When an overall opinion cannot be given, the reasons therefore should be provided (AICPA, 1994). To afford a reasonable basis for an opinion regarding the financial statements under audit, sufficient competent evidential matter is to be obtained through inspection, observation, inquiries, and confirmations. Working papers should contain sufficient information to enable an experienced auditor having no previous connection with the audit to ascertain the evidence that supports the auditors' significant conclusions and judgments (GAO, 1994).

Financial-Related Audit Procedures

Developed to meet objectives of specific audits (Tierney, 1996), financial-related audit procedures are different from those of financial statement audits. At the outset of a financial-related audit, a preliminary survey must be conducted to research the history of the police program, activity, or function under audit. Areas to be audited in detail are then identified during this survey. Auditors should establish the criteria against which performance will be assessed and discuss them with those arranging for the audit as a part of the preliminary survey. They need also to develop detailed scope for the financial-related audit to be made up of selected parts of a police agency, e.g., a revenue or expenditures statement; budget to actual performance; specified controls and reporting for a program, contract, or grant, etc. The concluding effort of this phase should be focused on preparation of an audit plan and audit programs, which must be reduced to writing.

Once the audit plan and audit programs are in place, auditors must make specific tests to determine the allowability or unallowability of direct and indirect costs actually incurred, claimed under or charged to, and reimbursement sought by the police. The police are especially subjected to these tests after they become grantees of state or federal funds. The auditors' opinion on financial-related tests will, of course, be of great utility for financial decisions. Seldom, however, is a police program subjected to only a financial audit. The objectives of financial-related audits might require an assessment of achievement by the police after they receive state or federal funds. Audits to assess operating effectiveness or program achievement or results may not have dollar accountability as the primary audit objective.

Auditors must consider carefully the objectives for which an audit is undertaken, the use of the information an audit is to generate, and the effects the reported information is likely to have on the users. One common audit objective may be to find out whether a budgeted level of performance has been accomplished or whether the expected performance has been achieved for the money spent. The bottom line is that audit information used as the basis for such decisions as future funding, program reduction or expansion, and quality of program performance must provide information relevant to these concerns (Tierney, 1996).

Performance Audit Procedures

Performance audit procedures are similar to as well as different from financial audit procedures. On the one hand, some audit methodology is transferable from financial audits to performance audits. Performance audits also require the application of the same skills, disciplines, ethical restraints, independence, and competence as financial audits. On the other hand, performance audits are in sharp contrast to financial statement audits because performance audits are not conducted annually, not primarily based on validating past practices, not exclusively concerned with amounts posted in an accounting system, and do not conclude with a standard, single-paragraph audit opinion (Tierney, 1996). As Knighton (1967) pointed out, a performance audit places greater emphasis on evaluating current and contemplated practices than on validating historical information. This emphasis often leads to development of techniques and strategies for change in police organization and operations (Cox, 1992).

The focus of performance audits on analysis of current practices also brings them closer to social scientific research methods used in evaluating police programs and functions. As Tierney (1996) said, although accountants are credited with creating performance audits, social scientists practice this method of analysis just as much. Over the years, a blending of the scientific methods of rigorous social research with the documentation and evidence gathering discipline of auditing has produced the most successful performance audits (Knighton, 1967; Tierney, 1996). The research methods social researchers use such as observations, surveys, and interviews have been commonly used in performance audits.

As a variety of methods is available for performance auditing, there is a variety of performance audits that have been completed. Performance audits are designed to address the objectives of those who arrange for them, and the types of performance audits vary in direct proportion to those desiring such audits. There is simply no single technique that represents the best practice in performance auditing. The methods and focus of a performance audit are directly dependent upon the police organization being audited, the nature of police operations, and the objectives of the audit. Different methods are required for gathering different kinds of data in order for the auditors to define and understand various elements of the organization such as attitudes, culture, and environment. Different programs or attributes of the organization also require separate examinations and special analytical techniques. The auditors, faced with a variety of methods to choose from, may opt to use multiple methods in combination to enhance their understanding of a certain aspect of the police organization (Cox, 1992). Police operating procedures, for example, can best be understood through a review of the police files and documents, a random survey of police officers, personal interviews, and field observations. Multiple procedures produce a more realistic picture of the operating procedures being reviewed than any of these methods used separately.

A performance audit begins with a decision to conduct such an audit. Cox (1992) discussed several situations where the decision for a performance audit could be made. It can be made because of intuition, as a result of changes in a police department, or as a routine practice. All things being considered, incorporating the performance audit as a planned, routine activity is the best approach. Unfortunately, this approach is not always feasible because few police departments have the fiscal or human resources for routine performance audits. The next best way to attempt such an effort is at the time when other changes in a police department are being planned such as a reorganization or leadership change. The reality for this approach is that resources are devoted to such a project only during times of crisis and when the problems are apparent to all. The narrow focus of a crisis-driven audit limits its value to the specific problems at hand. Once the crisis is resolved, the management team is little better informed about the overall effectiveness of the management practices.

After the decision to conduct a performance audit is made, agency officials or an audit organization will identify the nature of skills needed and select auditors with those skills to carry out the audit. Skills required for police audits usually include expertise other than accounting and auditing such as organizational diagnosis, program evaluation, and community survey. What skills are needed depends on the situation a police organization or program is in. An audit of a local police department, for example, will require knowledge of the local law enforcement statutes and standards, while an audit of a federally-funded community policing program will require familiarity with the Violent Crime Control and Law Enforcement Act of 1994 and related federal statutes and guidelines.

Performance audit process usually consists of five major phases or types of activities: (1) pre-audit phase, which consists of audit orientation, background survey, and audit planning; (2) audit phase, which includes gathering of competent, sufficient, and relevant evidence; (3) analysis phase, which involves developing and analyzing findings from the audit evidence; (4) recommendation and report phase, which entails making and presenting recommendations for changing deficient practices; and (5) implementation phase, which requires implementing recommendations and making changes. The rest of this chapter is devoted to a discussion of these activities.

First, the pre-audit phase includes audit orientation, background survey, and audit planning. An initial, pre-audit meeting with police management and staff should be held for the purposes of introduction and orientation, during which those arranging for the audit and the auditors should establish specific agreements or understandings between them (Tierney, 1996). The auditors should arrange with the police at this time for access to the organization, make a full presentation of the contemplated scope, confirm the objectives of the audit, provide copies of review protocols, and give a briefing on the various phases of the audit. Audit orientation as well as the later audit activities will be carried out more smoothly if auditors consider the political and human environment in which the audit is to take place and the responsibilities accepted by police management in the conduct of their business. Dittenhofer (1997: Chap. 22) described a concept called "participative auditing," which is a useful technique for dealing with the political and human factors that, if handled poorly, may prove detrimental to performance auditing.

Participative auditing is a partnership between the police auditor and the audited agency established at the beginning of a performance audit to facilitate the auditing process. During the entrance conference with the police, the auditor utilizing this technique describes the work to be performed, introduces the audit staff, and asks the police officials about any specific areas that should be audited. The auditor explains that, if there are any findings, they will be immediately reported to the police and that the audit report will make several statements of cooperation between the auditor and the police such as the following: The examination of the particular area was made at the police administration's suggestion or request; the situation disclosed by the audit was discussed with the police management, alternative resolutions were jointly explored, and an optimum resolution was jointly selected; the audited agency has implemented or is in the process of implementing the resolution procedure recommended; and the auditee evidenced a cooperative attitude and helped to conduct a successful audit. This approach results in the police being credited for being aware of actual or potential trouble spots, for using good managerial judgment in the solution of the problems disclosed by the audit, and for cooperating through the prompt installation of corrective measures. The technique has been used successfully in government audits and resulted in requests from operating officials for audits to assist them in the management of their organizations. As Mints (1972) indicated, it is an outstanding example of the use of practical behavioral techniques to strengthen auditing and improve management.

Once initial agreements or understandings are reached, auditors should quickly conduct a background survey to compile and analyze initial historical, background, operating, and financial data (GAO, 1988). The purpose of a background survey is to obtain an overview of the audited agency and some indication of the structure, activities, functions, operations, or other subjects that may require more detailed examination later on in the audit. Critical audit decisions will be made after the survey on what is or is not subject to a detailed audit. The survey should also familiarize auditors with the organization, program, or function to be audited and enable them to describe the scope and objectives of the audit. In order to do so, auditors should reduce each audit objective to questions about specific aspects of the audited program such as purposes, goals, efforts, operations, outputs, and outcomes. The scope of a performance audit can be determined by examining the circumstances in which the audit is to be conducted and the product that is expected, or by identifying the causes of current performance problems and deficiencies (Cox, 1992).

Furthermore, background survey should enable auditors to ascertain the extent to which performance criteria and operational, managerial, and financial data are available and the extent that the lack of such criteria and data might limit the desired scope of a performance audit or demand more time, staff, and/or other resources. Performance audits require that particular attention be paid to determining and establishing quantifiable performance criteria. Establishing appropriate performance criteria is an essential element in audit planning, and auditors must give careful consideration to selecting these criteria in order to measure agency performance accurately and aid police management in their decision-making. A performance audit should, for example, establish that suitable criteria exist for data collection and analysis of criminal and noncriminal events. Crime analysis based on these criteria can then be used to allocate and deploy patrol resources. The quality and utility of crime analysis, therefore, depend on these criteria; and police management's use of the crime analysis results also depends on these criteria (Rabenhorst, 1997: Chap. 34).

In addition to quantitative criteria, performance auditors must give weight to qualitative criteria as well in assessing relative materiality and significance. GAO (1994) has suggested several qualitative factors, such as the visibility and sensitivity of the program under audit, new-ness of the program or changes in its conditions, and role of the audit in providing information that can be used to improve police account-ability and decision-making. Program visibility and sensitivity are often equated to the interest expressed by news media and other inter-est groups capable of influencing legislative and executive officials. New and changed programs are of interest to both proponents and opponents who have probably established performance or evaluative criteria at least to their own satisfaction. Performance auditors should be particularly critical to police programs lacking any performance cri-teria that can be used to measure their efficiency and effectiveness. As Drucker (1973) observed, the lack of efficiency and effectiveness tests might put an inefficient, obsolete, unproductive, or nonresponsive business-type operation out of business.

The government performance auditing standards require that per-formance criteria be determined only after acquiring a familiarity with several interrelated factors, including laws and regulations, manage-ment policies, objectives and goals, police activities and program oper-ations, and outputs and outcomes. The legislation establishing a police agency or program and records of legislative hearings have often pre-scribed or indicated purposes or goals for the audited agency or pro-gram. General objectives and goals may also be obtained from policies and procedures issued by agency management for particular pro-grams. If the enabling legislation, policies, or relevant information ex-ist, police auditors can utilize the objectives and related information as criteria for purposes of measuring or assessing police performance. Auditors may also use agency plans and policies established to imple-ment legislation and meet constituent needs as measurement criteria because agency management may have already established operating policies and procedures consistent with the enabling legislation. And financial and management information systems and controls may have been designed to monitor and measure progress or achievement in relationship to goals or objectives in the law (Tierney, 1996).

Unfortunately, auditors may not always find information that can be used as measurement criteria in performance auditing. Some police departments may not have clear legal mandates with financial, operational, or constituent bases. In many cases, agencies have not formulated goals or objectives for their operations. In many others, agencies have attempted formulating goals and objectives, but their goals and objectives tend to be vague, characteristically unquantifiable, and lacking in qualitative precision. When clearly specified or quantifiable goals and objectives are unavailable or there is a dearth of guidance on the intended purpose of a police program, an auditor may become responsible for developing that database as a precedent condition to planning the performance audit. This may prove to be a performance auditor's most difficult task (Tierney, 1996; Malan, 1997: Chap. 30), which usually involves searching for proxies that could be used for establishing performance measures.

Possible proxies auditors can use in developing performance measurement criteria may be obtained from available literature applicable to the function being audited because police professional associations have developed adequate criteria against which agency performance can be measured. Other possible proxies for performance criteria or indicators include technically developed standards, norms, and levels that might be based on prudence and "common sense"; expert opinions within the program area or subjects relevant to program operations; prior year's performances; comparisons to earlier proposals, budgets, and plans; and performance information from comparable police agencies in similar circumstances and under similar restrictions.

Auditors may also find it helpful to ask a series of questions as they develop performance measurement criteria. What types of police services are offered? When or with what frequency is the service provided? What is the pricing structure for the police services? Are prices perceived reasonable for the services to various constituents? Are total costs of police operations and services known and periodically reviewed? Are police budgets sufficient to cover police operating costs?

Are other financial sources or subsidies used to support operating cost or capital investments? Are the reported costs all inclusive—has any cost been underreported or deferred to future periods? Are constituents relatively satisfied with the frequency and type of police services provided? Should the services be expanded? Are the services provided and sources of financial support consistent with state and local laws and statutes and federal legislation and regulations? Have agency, program, activity, or functional objectives and goals been well defined? Have specific timetables or dates been established for meeting the objectives and goals? Have criteria—in terms of performance levels or costs—been established to permit the evaluation of results or achievements? Have the criteria been quantified to permit objective measurement of results or achievements? Have arrangements been made to insure that this data will be available to the auditor? Has management or someone else prepared a current assessment of the police program's results or achievements? Have any previous external evaluations been made of the police agency, program, or activities being audited? Have actions been taken by police management as a result of these previous evaluations? Evidence, data, information, or answers related to these questions would permit auditors to understand more clearly the nature of the performance audit, to structure more appropriately the audit plan, and eventually to develop more specifically the performance measurement criteria.

Auditors should always seek to identify and develop performance measurement criteria that will help them report most directly the results of police operations for the program being audited, especially those related to accomplishing the goals and objectives of the program. Researchers associated with the Government Accounting Standards Board have conducted some investigation into the topic of police measurement criteria (Hatry, Fountain, Sullivan, & Kremer, 1990) by examining the extent to which quantified goals and objectives have been developed and used by police services. Their findings suggest that the state of the art in police performance measurement criteria has developed sufficiently to warrant their use in audits or external reports of police services. Focusing on these criteria in reporting accountability information and monitoring police performance, auditors can determine if there have been any improvements in efficiency and effectiveness in accomplishing program goals and objectives. Auditing reports with the use of these criteria should allow readers to compare current results with benchmarks such as service effort and accomplishment indicators used in previous years, performance targets identified in police budgets and documents, comparable data collected in comparable jurisdictions, established norms or standards reflecting what is considered an acceptable level of performance, and the jurisdiction-wide average.

Four types of performance measurement criteria, i.e., input, output, outcome, and efficiency (including cost-effectiveness) along with explanatory variables can be used in performance auditing. Input indicates the level of material, financial, and human resources consumed by the police program, and types, frequency, and duration of police activities supported by these resources. Output measures whether the police have achieved objectives set for their programs or functions. Outcome indicates the impact of their program and accomplishments of their goals. Efficiency measures provide an indication of the cost efficiency of police efforts and an indication of the productivity of personnel in providing police services. Explanatory variables provide information on factors that are likely to affect the incident and effects of criminal activity so that measures of output, outcome, and efficiency can be viewed in a proper context (Drebin & Brannon, 1990). These criteria fit the purpose of performance audit because an important purpose of using performance criteria is to demonstrate to those groups that a police department is held accountable to that it has achieved or fulfilled its responsibilities. Due to the variety of police functions, however, specific definitions of these criteria may be different from program to program.

Although preparatory audit activities discussed heretofore may be cumbersome and tedious to perform, audits with some investment of time in them will prove more cost-efficient than those without. With a good understanding of audit scope and objectives, auditors will know where to collect the data and what data to collect during the audit phase. With access to and cooperation from the police, auditors may be able to eliminate or reduce some of the political and human obstacles inherent in the auditing process. With the performance criteria clearly established, they will find it possible to interpret and analyze the information collected in a manner acceptable to consumers of the audit report. These pre-audit activities will eventually enable auditors to refine their audit plan and develop detailed audit programs that provide direction to auditing specific areas of risk.

Second, the audit phase entails gathering of competent, sufficient, and relevant evidence to confirm the performance audit. The currency, completeness, accuracy, relevancy, and underlying validity of all audit information must be determined during this phase so that audit findings can be developed and crystallized for reporting. The overall objective of this phase is to identify those problem areas that warrant attention of police management and/or other overseer groups. Auditors are usually critical, therefore, in their investigation of police practices and tend to compile data on current police deficiencies. To avoid potential bias in their investigation and maintain independence in processing a wide variety of data, auditors should collect information against performance criteria established in the pre-audit phase, employ multiple data collection techniques, and use multiple sources of information. The collection of evidence according to performance criteria determined at the pre-audit phase is critical when various and controversial criteria can be used to measure the same police service. Multiple methods by which data can be collected and confirmed may include system review, document examination, statistical sampling, model development, questionnaire survey, interview protocol, personal observation, written confirmation, and external testimony (Tierney, 1996). The evidence to be gathered could equally be comprised of financial, statistical, and operational data or judgments, opinions, and perceptions held by legislators, police officials, and the constituents served by the police.

Because the search for evidence on the operations of a police agency can seem overwhelming, it would be best for auditors to follow the scope and objectives of an audit (Norbeck, 1969; Brown, Gallagher, & Williams, 1982). The scope and objectives of a performance audit usually cover goals and objectives of police programs, and auditors should collect evidence on whether the police have met them. The goals for patrols, for example, can be broadly stated as providing emergency services, increasing quality of life, preventing crime, repressing crime, apprehending offenders, and recovering property. Specific patrol services may include domestic violence response teams, community crime prevention programs, hot-spot patrol activities, team policing, specialized policing, and problem-oriented policing

(Rabenhorst, 1997: Chap. 34). Within the scope and objectives of an audit as well as goals and objectives of an audited program, auditors will find themselves better positioned in collecting information concerning police performance and in identifying and quantifying the nature of services provided, increases or decreases in service levels, frequency and quality of services delivered, constituencies served, changes in costing and financing needs, decreased backlogs, increased error rates, financial and other budgetary resources, other performance statistics, and activity trend and volume indicators (Tierney, 1996). They will also be able to have a better understanding of specific issues at hand, for example, whether police officers are distributed to patrol sectors as efficiently as possible, given the expected level of incident reports; whether appropriate work standards are used to ensure that fleet management is performed efficiently and effectively; whether the system for calling police officers to court for testimony is cost-effective; and whether a department's purchasing activity uses a fair process to ensure that the agency receive the necessary quality at the best possible price.

Police audit data should be largely quantitative to facilitate data management and analysis although qualitative data is indispensable in measuring those efforts and effects that are unquantifiable. Since police have standards and routine procedures in record keeping, quantitative data derived from existing logs and reports are often readily available. In fact, a variety of statistics concerning police operations exists in police agencies. In the area of patrol, for example, a great amount of statistics exists that can be used to demonstrate how patrol resources are used to fulfill police functions. These data include percent of total patrol time spent in response to calls; record of officer availability in response to emergency calls; response time; length of time for handling various types of calls; number of call-backs preceding on-scene response; pattern and attributed causes of traffic accidents, property damage, or personal injury; pattern of officer actions in cases of noncriminal violations; count and pattern of vandalism, property destruction, and other crimes; count of on-scene arrests in response to service calls; count of arrests resulting from preventive patrols; count of reported crimes undetected in patrolled areas; record of arrests of known suspects caught in a criminal act through surveillance, and change in statistics for crimes attributable to incarcerated suspects; count of arrests from information original patrol officers developed; and record of owner-marked property recovered through investigation (Rabenhorst, 1997: Chap. 34).

A communication audit of a major UK policing body with over 12,000 officers generated comprehensive and detailed information about a wide range of issues surrounding communication (Quinn, Hargie, & Tourish, 2009). The audit utilized three tools for data collection, namely, face-to-face interviews and two separate questionnaires. One of the questionnaires was an adaptation of the International Communication Audit (ICA) Survey (Goldhaber and Rogers, 1979) employed to measure communication in general. At the end of the questionnaire, subjects were requested to record details of one communication incident, whether effective or ineffective, and were asked to provide suggestions as to how communication could be improved. The other questionnaire was the Organizational Culture Survey (Glaser, Zamanou, & Hacker, 1987). A quota sample of 20 percent of officers (n = 41) within one subdivision was selected with each interview lasting 35–40 minutes. The sample spanned the hierarchical levels from constable to inspector.

In addition to data internal to the police agency, performance auditors often need to collect information from the community to gauge the effect of police programs especially when the programs are intended to achieve a certain impact on the community. Periodic independent surveys should be conducted on community attitudes about the police programs, and the results should be interpreted along with other measures of police activities used in the audit. The extent to which citizens are involved in certain activities may also indicate community attitudes toward their local police. Community involvement can take the forms of joint projects with the police, volunteer or auxiliary police capacity, block associations, and information exchange with the police. Some forms of community involvement such as resident patrols are of special interest to police auditors because they can extend police preventive patrols at almost no cost to the police and the constituents. The police, in order to meet their patrol objectives more efficiently and effectively, should work with community groups to coordinate resident patrols, establish channels of communications, set standards for reporting occurrences, and provide necessary training and support (Rabenhorst, 1997: Chap. 34).

The audit phase is where auditors have the most direct contact with agency personnel due to their on-site data collection activities. Auditors should be aware that performance auditing is conducted usually in a politically charged and behaviorally complex environment, and adversarial auditee activities intended to discourage the auditors from pursuing their objectives may make auditing difficult and in some cases outright impossible. Examples of such activities include showing disinterest in the audit, reluctance to provide information or documentation, accusing auditors of interference and poor audit practices, and aggressively rejecting audit activities (Dittenhofer, 1997: Chap. 22). It is crucial for auditors to work professionally and ethically with the police in order to obtain valid and reliable data.

In order to ensure successful audit operations, police management must be extended all possible courtesy and consideration and advised periodically of audit progress (Malan, 1997: Chap. 30). Participative auditing established during the pre-audit phase can help auditors obtain police cooperation and address adversarial activities if any occurs. Participative auditing can be practiced only, however, when auditors have credibility as to their ethical and professional conduct. Acceptance of audit activities and later findings depend largely on how well police executives understand the performance audit function and recognize its validity. Their understanding and recognition should increase if they are convinced of the credibility of the audit staff. As Malan (1997: Chap. 30) pointed out, it is essential that the performance audit function be grounded firmly in professional competence.

Auditing has an operational impact and people's receptivity to an audit can result in greater cooperation. Dittenhofer (1997: Chap. 22) believed that considering the impact of some basic behavioral principles can result in improved audit efforts. Performance auditors should consider the human relations or behavioral aspects of performance auditing. When motivated, police officers will provide support and effort that aid materially in carrying out audit intentions. Behavioral issues include various elements of applied psychology such as listening; the management of stress, conflict, and change; the effect of fear on action and inaction; motivation; behavioral dynamics; and communicating through reporting. In many cases, the behavioral aspects are known to the auditor but are not applied consciously to his or her professional work.

Third, audit analysis involves developing and analyzing audit findings. In this phase of performance auditing, data on police services and programs collected in the previous phase are evaluated as to their relative economy, efficiency, effectiveness, and results in order to ascertain whether a reportable condition exists. A technique to ensure that a reportable and significant condition exists is to critically examine audit evidence in support of all elements of a finding, which include condition, criteria, cause, effect, and conclusions. Condition refers to the situations, circumstances, or practices that have been identified as contributing to less than desired results. Criteria are the objectives, goals, standards, laws, regulations, rules, or other guidelines that are not being achieved or with which there are instances of noncompliance. Cause involves the contributory circumstances or practices that have resulted in the less than desired condition or results. Effect is the relative materiality, damage, or cost of impairment or loss resulting from the existence or perpetuation of the less than desired condition or results. And conclusions are the auditor's opinion or assessment or attestation to the conditions that have been identified as contributing to the less than desired condition or results (GAO, 1988).

Similarly, auditors can develop and analyze their findings in light of input, output, outcome, and efficiency indicators, all of which are relatively verifiable. When considering the indicators involved, auditors should perform verification to the level necessary for management use. As the technical capabilities of auditors increase in performing the verification, the level of verification will also increase, especially for indicators used for performance evaluation and resource allocation. Auditors, however, must use caution when using these indicators because their utility can be severely limited by problems of measurement validity and reliability (Drebin & Brannon, 1990). Measurement problems are a serious concern for performance auditors because of diversity of police responsibilities and sharing of resources among different programs.

The commonly recognized police responsibilities include prevention of criminal activity; detection of criminal activity; apprehension of criminal offenders; participation in court proceedings; protection of constitutional guarantees; assistance to those who cannot care for themselves or who are in danger of physical harm; control of traffic; resolution of day-to-day conflicts among family, friends, and neighbors; creation and maintenance of a feeling of security in the community; and promotion and preservation of civil order (National Advisory Commission on Criminal Justice Standards and Goals, 1973). Because of the diversity of police functions, measures of performance in various areas are not likely to be comparable. Different police services may share the same resources. Patrol resources, for example, are directed toward traffic as well as crime. Because of sharing of resources among different police programs, any findings about these programs must be viewed in light of such relationships (Drebin & Brannon, 1990).

It is important, therefore, to examine not only output and outcome or effect produced by personnel directly involved in certain police operations, but also input, conditions, and contributory factors involving personnel participating indirectly in these operations. In case of measuring criminal investigation activities, for example, auditors should not only analyze increases in those variables that indicate the efforts of detectives such as number of arrests, rate of acceptance of cases for prosecution, and percent of convictions for serious crimes, but also the efforts of those other than detectives that have contributed to the increases of these variables. Coordination with patrol officers apparently enhances the effectiveness of criminal investigation. Improved relationship with the patrol function benefits criminal investigation because patrol officers provide information to detectives that often leads to arrests. Auditors need to analyze the rate of arrests due to patrol officer information to pinpoint the relationship between investigators and patrol officers and measure their joint effectiveness (Rabenhorst, 1997: Chap. 34). Coordination with prosecutors also improves the effectiveness of criminal investigators. Data to assess their relationship include number and types of cases accepted for prosecution, elapsed time between arrest date and conference with prosecutors, number of meetings with prosecutors, number of cases incorporating prosecution feedback, and number of prosecutor-checklist items completed during investigation. In addition, screening procedures used in determining cases to be assigned can affect the investigative workload and the ability to initiate investigations promptly. To determine the efficiency and responsiveness of investigators, records should be maintained of the number of cases suspended within and after one month of assignment, ratio of closures to total cases assigned, and average investigative time spent on cases closed and cases suspended (Rabenhorst, 1997: Chap. 34).

Developing and analyzing findings with established performance indicators is not always a straightforward process. In *Service Efforts and Accomplishment Reports,* Drebin and Brannon (1990) illustrated the difficulties and need to be cautious in using input, output, outcome, and efficiency measures in analyzing crime-related police activities. Input measures for crime-related activities include expenditures; equipment, facilities, and vehicles; and number of personnel and hours expended. Expenditures are considered the most valid indicator of efforts expended in crime-related activities, and any outcomes must be viewed in relationship to resource commitment. The primary difficulty lies in how to measure expenditures due to the many common costs associated with different police functions. Auditors need to use or develop accounting and budgeting techniques to overcome this difficulty. Information about equipment, facilities, and vehicles indicates the size and scope of the department and resources devoted to police service, but is not meant to demonstrate how efficiently or effectively these resources have been used to achieve departmental objectives. Auditors should report the dollar cost of equipment used in crime-related activities only because cost figures provide some degree of comparability among different jurisdictions and time periods. The validity of such a figure is affected by such factors as inflation and regional cost differences. Police departments also measure personnel and hours expended in a variety of ways. Some report the number of employees, which could be misleading as some employees work less than full time. For auditing purposes, the number of personnel hours required to complete a given task is a more relevant measure because personnel-hours provides a base measure of the human resources used in crime-related activities. The measure is readily comparable among jurisdictions and years, and is not affected by cost variations. In order to make comparisons over time or with similar jurisdictions, the measure should be considered over the budgetary time period, i.e., personnel-hours expended per year. Reporting the number of officers per thousand population might seem to lend itself to comparisons between cities. But the makeup of the population may be quite different, and the expanse of the area to cover for the same-size population may vary greatly. The number of businesses in and visitors to the community are not taken into account by this measure, either (Hatry, 1977).

Output measures for crime-related police activities include hours of patrol, miles patrolled, responses to calls for service, crimes investigated, number of arrests made and warrants served, and crime prevention activities. These indicators have the advantage of being objectively determinable and thus suitable for auditing. They represent the direct outputs of police activities and are important in evaluating accomplishments. The problem with them is that they do not indicate directly why a police department is performing these services and whether departmental objectives have been met. Hours and miles of patrol data should be disaggregated according to communities served to help determine quality and equitable distribution of service. The number of calls for service provides an indication of the demand for police assistance in the community, but calls for service and calls involving crime should be separated and crime-related calls should be further broken down by type of crimes for the purpose of auditing crime-related activities. The report of crimes investigated should include not only the number of investigations but also the amount of time involved in the investigation process to avoid the problem of encouraging concentration of efforts on simple cases while ignoring complex ones. Also, crimes should be categorized based on the relative need for and potential value of investigation to keep the police from reporting a single incident or offender as multiple crimes. The number of arrests can be related to the number of crimes investigated to indicate a level of success in criminal investigation activities. One problem in using the arrest data is the comparability of units used with other proposed measures. For example, the definition of clearance permits only one clearance for each crime, regardless of how many arrests are made. For this reason, potential users of these figures should be aware that the totals are not comparable. Arrest data should also be disaggregated by type of crime to provide some sense of direction a department is headed to, and to indicate the degree of success in apprehending suspects involved in particular types of crimes. Arrest data should be further broken down by geographical area and demographic character of the suspect and arrestee. Crime prevention activities can be measured possibly by the number of crime prevention presentations made, number of community participants present, and other quantifiable or objective data related to this effort. However, because so many variables are likely to affect crime, it is almost impossible to ascribe a causal relationship to crime prevention activities.

Crime-related outcome measures may involve response time, citizen complaints, citizen satisfaction, deaths and bodily injury resulting from a crime, value of property lost, crimes committed, and crime clearance. Response time, citizen complaints, and citizen satisfaction are quality measures as they indicate the quality of police service. When using response time, auditors should be aware that a simple average response time may not be the most relevant information. A better measure is the percentage of responses below a predetermined critical limit and data classified according to relevance to crime or other services and further broken down by urgency and location. It is quite difficult to measure objectively what are serious and minor injuries. The police should consider limiting the measure of number of injuries to those involving admission to a hospital, or estimate the number of days of productive activity lost due to injury. The difficulty with the property loss measure is obtaining objective data to estimate its magnitude. Many property crimes that do not involve insurance claims go unreported. Police often report recoveries without netting them against the loss figures to provide an indication of the effect of the crime. Adjusting figures by a price index such as the Consumer Price Index would make year-to-year comparisons more meaningful. Since reported crimes are not always an accurate measure of the outcome of police activity, victimization surveys should be conducted periodically to provide a means of assessing the validity of the reported crime data. Since the relationship between police activities and outcomes is critical to evaluating police effectiveness, disaggregation of crimes committed to reflect those that are likely to be affected by police intervention would provide more relevant information.

Efficiency measures include cost per case assigned, cost per crime cleared, and personnel-hours per crime cleared. These measures provide an indication of the cost efficiency of police efforts and an indication of the productivity of personnel in providing police services. Input measures such as expenditures, equipment, facilities, and number of personnel hours expended can be combined with output or outcome measures to develop ratios that indicate how efficiently or effectively services are provided with resource constraints.

In addition to input, output, outcome, and efficiency indicators used to measure crime-related police activities, Drebin and Brannon (1990) discussed the necessity of using explanatory variables to isolate the effect of police actions from other factors, or disaggregate direct measures from indirect ones. Explanatory variables help auditors and

audit report users understand the environment in which the police service is delivered and the factors that may have affected the results of
that service. The explanatory variables will differ from agency to agency
and between jurisdictions and should be classified as to the extent to
which the police affect them. Explanatory variables related to crime-
related police activities include population by age group, unemployment rate, number of households, number of businesses, percentage of
population below poverty level, land area, dollar value of property
within a jurisdiction, demand for service, and cases assigned. These
factors can also be used to develop ratios that place different police
jurisdictions on a comparable basis and thus help interpret data because ratios are necessary to place different jurisdictions on the same
scale. Two ratios that are widely used are crimes per thousand population (crimes committed divided by population) and clearance rates
(crimes cleared divided by number of crimes).

Each audit finding developed in this phase should be based on
careful and critical analysis of all elements of the evidence that supports the finding. The auditors should not assume, however, that audit
findings developed by examining all aspects of the information such
as input, output, outcome, and efficiency will be readily acceptable to
the police or other interested parties. Because of the political nature of
auditing, police management should be shown the audit findings and
analyses before they are released to the public and given the opportunity to respond to them. Nonetheless, the understanding of the political nature of the auditing process does not mean that police management should be given the opportunity or put in a position to influence
the outcome of an audit or politicize the audit function (Malan, 1997:
Chap. 30).

The fourth phase includes audit recommendations and audit report. Recommendation activities involve developing strategies for changing deficient police practices. The recommendations should be based
on audit findings and analysis results obtained from the previous
phase. In case of patrol, for instance, the results of the data analysis
should be used in making recommendations on patrol resource allocation and deployment (Rabenhorst, 1997: Chap. 34).

Before auditors make their recommendations, however, they
should follow up on known material findings and recommendations
from previous audits to see whether prior recommendations have been

implemented and/or have produced any positive results. Understanding why some recommendations have not been implemented or whether previous recommendations have benefited the police, auditors may be able to provide more informed and feasible recommendations.

As during the phase of audit data collection, auditors should make their recommendations within the scope and objectives of an audit and according to the measurement criteria established in the pre-audit phase. If the audit scope and objectives are too broad or definitions of the measurement criteria too liberal, auditors will face the problems of losing focus on important audit issues and not being able to accomplish anything worthwhile. On the other hand, if the pre-audit conditions are too restrictive, auditors may find themselves constrained in their ability to make any meaningful recommendations. It is important to strike a balance between the two extremes considering the many facets of police auditing. While most of the recommendations should be concerned with the internal police management and operations, auditors do find it necessary occasionally to have the ability to suggest changes of related policies or practices in the municipal government in which the police operate. If the scope of the audit allows the auditors to provide recommendations not only to the police but also related government agencies, they can identify the necessary support required, such as financial, material, and human resources, from other municipal government agencies and recommend their support. These types of recommendations may be critical to the police because local police agencies do not usually have control over their financial and human resources. Many police programs are also dependent upon collaboration with other government programs.

Recommendations, when presented to the police and other concerned government agencies, should be contained in the final audit reports along with audit findings and analyses. Although there are no standard structures or formats for reporting the results of performance audits, performance audit reports must be responsive to specific objectives of the engagement and provide the results of the audit in an agreed-upon format. Eventually, the performance report must be distributed to the party arranging for the audit, officials responsible for taking actions, the audited police agency, state or federal financing departments and agencies, legislators and others authorized to receive the report, and, if of interest, the general public and the news media.

The fifth and last phase of performance audit involves implementation activities. In most cases, the audit mission is accomplished as soon as auditors complete the fourth phase and present the audit report. Police administration will then be responsible for implementing the audit recommendations. It is desirable, however, to extend performance auditors' duties and responsibilities beyond the audit reporting phase. Auditors can play the role of evaluators or monitors of the implementation process. If they are not available for this role, other professional evaluators independent of the police should be employed to track how audit recommendations are implemented. This stage of the auditing process is important because the benefit from audit work is not in the findings reported or the recommendations made, but in their effective resolution. An auditor or an audit organization's effectiveness should be measured not only by the types of issues it tackles but also the changes and improvements it is able to effect (GAO, 1994). In patrol, for example, evidence of increased patrol effectiveness resulting from the use of patrol recommendations can be gathered in this phase to evaluate police effectiveness in implementing the recommendations and the effectiveness of the auditors in bringing about desired changes (Rabenhorst, 1997: Chap. 34).

SUMMARY

Audit procedures are acts performed or steps taken by auditors in conducting an audit. Auditors usually begin their audit by performing a pre-audit survey to obtain background information regarding a police organization, program, or function. They then plan the audit and develop an audit program that will guide them through the audit process and ensure that they reach their objectives without wasted time. With the audit plan and audit program in place, auditors gather relevant evidence with a variety of data collection techniques. They analyze the evidence collected and develop findings based on systematic analysis. Finally, they make recommendations according to the findings and write the audit report.

Auditors conducting the three major types of police audits, i.e., financial statement, financial-related, and performance, follow similar general procedures or steps, but do not focus on the same issues or use the same methods. The specific procedures are different when applied to these audits and auditors engage in them with different purposes and objectives. The procedures for financial statement audits are mandated by generally accepted government as well as corporate auditing standards. They involve substantive audit tests and procedures performed to obtain evidence to support various financial statement assertions. These substantive tests for financial statement audits are detailed tests conducted of classes of transactions and account balances and analytical review procedures. Financial-related audit procedures are different from financial statement audit procedures because they are developed to meet specific objectives of each audit. Financial-related auditors oftentimes must consider the unique objectives of the audit undertaken and how the audit information will be used. They make specific tests to determine the allowability and unallowability of direct and indirect costs actually incurred, claimed under or charged to, and reimbursement sought by the police according to audit objectives. Financial-related audits may also involve assessment of operating effectiveness or program achievement in which the dollar accountability would be regarded as a subsidiary objective.

Different from financial type of police audits, performance audits place greater emphasis on analyses of current and contemplated practices than on validation of historical information. This emphasis should eventually lead to development of techniques and strategies for changing and improving police practices. Due to the goal of bringing about positive changes in the audited police agency, performance auditors must pay greater attention to issues involving audit scope and objectives, performance measurement criteria, and the political and behavioral environment in which the audit is to be conducted. Without these considerations, auditors will not be able to collect appropriate data, conduct accurate analysis of gathered evidence, and make objective and feasible recommendations. Because performance audits are designed to address concerns of those that have arranged for them, the methodology and focus of each performance audit may vary in direct proportion to the demands of those desiring such audits.

REFERENCES

AICPA. (1994). *Audit and accounting guide: Audits of state and local governmental units.* Section 18.34. New York: American Institute of Certified Public Accounts.

Brown, R. E., Gallagher, T. P., & Williams, M. C. (1982). *Auditing performance in government.* New York: John Wiley.

Cox, R. W. (1992). Managerial concepts of control of the organization: The management audit. In H. W. More & P. C. Unsinger (Eds.), *Managerial control of the police: Internal affairs and audits.* Springfield, IL: Charles C Thomas.

Dittenhofer, M. A. (1997). Chapter 22. In M. A. Dittenhofer & E. W. Stepnick (Eds.), *Applying government auditing standards.* New York: Matthew Bender.

Drebin, A., & Brannon, M. (1990). Police department programs. In H. P. Hatry, J. R. Fountain, J. M. Sullivan, & L. Kremer (Eds.), *Service efforts and accomplishments reporting: Its time has come.* Norwalk, CT: Government Accounting Standards Board of the Financial Accounting Foundation.

Drucker, P. F. (1973). *Management: Tasks, responsibilities, practices.* New York: Harper & Row.

General Accounting Office (GAO). (1988). *Government auditing standards.* Washington, D.C.: U.S. Government Printing Office.

General Accounting Office (GAO). (1994). *Government auditing standards.* Washington, D.C.: U.S. Government Printing Office.

Glaser, S., Zamanou, S., & Hacker, K. (1987). Measuring and interpreting organizational culture. *Management Communication Quarterly, 1,* 173–198.

Goldhaber, G., & Rogers, D. (1979). *Auditing organizational communication system: The ICA communication audit.* Dubuque, IA: Kendall/Hunt.

Hatry, H. P. (1977). *How effective are your community services? Procedures for measuring their quality.* Washington, D.C.: The Urban Institute and International City Management Association.

Hatry, H. P., Fountain, J. R., Sullivan, J. M., & Kremer L. (1990). *Service efforts and accomplishments reporting: Its time has come.* Norwalk, CT: Government Accounting Standards Board of Financial Accounting Foundation.

Knighton, L. M. (1967). *The performance post audit in state government: An analysis of its nature, its purpose, and its possibility.* East Lansing, MI: Michigan State University Press.

Malan, R. M. (1997). Chapter 30. In M. A. Dittenhofer & E. W. Stepnick (Eds.), *Applying government auditing standards.* New York: Matthew Bender.

Mints, F. (1972). *Behavioral patterns in internal audit relationships.* Altamonte Springs, FL: IIA.

National Advisory Commission on Criminal Justice Standards and Goals. (1973). *A national strategy to reduce crime.* Washington, D.C.: U.S. Government Printing Office.

Norbeck, E. (Ed.). (1969). *Operational auditing for management control.* New York: American Management Association.

Pickett, K. H. S. (2006). *Audit planning: A risk-based approach.* Hoboken, NJ: John Wiley & Sons.

Quinn, D., Hargie, O., & Tourish, D. (2009). Auditing a major police organization. In O. Hargie & D. Tourish (Eds.), *Auditing organizational communication: A handbook of research, theory and practice.* New York, NY: Routledge.

Rabenhorst, A. L. (1997). Chapter 34. In M. A. Dittenhofer & E. W. Stepnick (Eds.), *Applying government auditing standards.* New York: Matthew Bender.

Tierney, C. E. (1996). *Government auditing: Standards and practices.* Chicago: CCH.

Woolf, E., & Hindson, M. (2011). *Audit and accountancy pitfalls: A casebook for practicing accountants, lawyers and insurers.* Chichester, West Sussex, UK: John Wiley & Sons.

Chapter 5

VARIETY OF POLICE AUDITS

Theoretically and technically speaking, auditors must follow both the standards and procedures for financial statement, financial-related, and performance audits when conducting police audits. In the real world of auditing, however, auditors do not always specify the type of standards and procedures they use or the type of audits they do. Instead, they describe the audit activities they engage in and name their audits simply after the subject matters under investigation such as human resources, fleet management, use of force, and clearance rate, resulting in a variety of police audits. Consumers of audit reports often have to determine, as a result, the types of police audits completed by identifying the subject matter, activities, and methods of each specific audit and linking them to the generally accepted auditing standards and procedures. By doing so, audit readers should be able to recognize or categorize an audit as either a financial statement, financial-related, compliance, or performance audit. Because police auditing remains a discipline under development and usually addresses a particular issue in police management or operation, many police audits may not meet all the standards and procedures required in government auditing. Consequently, consumers of audit reports may have to judge the nature of each audit by considering the type of standards and procedures the audit matches most closely or by discerning the audit type the audit activities most resemble.

Most police audits that have been made available to the public focus on police compliance, economy, efficiency, and effectiveness, and should be considered therefore as compliance or performance audits. This does not mean that financial statement or financial-related audits are conducted less frequently in the police profession. Auditors do not publicize their financial statement audit reports as often because financial type of police audits are done routinely as an internal procedure. Also, the examination of financial aspects of police operations may be included in the performance audits. As discussed in the previous chapters, performance audits encompass those issues related to the economy and efficiency of the police agency; program results and effectiveness; and compliance with laws and regulations concerning matters of economy and efficiency and program results and effectiveness.

In this chapter, audits of various aspects of the police profession are sampled and discussed under several subheadings, i.e., financial-related audits, economy and efficiency audits, program results and effectiveness audits, efficiency and effectiveness audits combined, and compliance audits. The purpose of presenting police audits under these subheadings is to suggest that some audits have a stronger focus on one aspect of policing than another. Audits with an equal emphasis on two aspects of policing are categorized as "efficiency and effectiveness audits combined." Each audit type is illustrated by using several audit cases, and each case is presented by introducing the audit issues first, and then describing the audit methods, audit findings, and audit recommendations. Responses to audit recommendations are included if such information is available.

Financial-Related Audits

Financial statement audits provide reasonable assurance that the financial statements fairly present the financial position, results of operations, and cash flows of a police agency. Due to their focus on internal control, financial statement audits are seldom made available to the public. They are not included therefore as part of the presentation of audit cases in this chapter. Financial-related audits share the same general standards and procedures with financial statement audits, but report on selected programs or units of a police department. The two financial-related audits described below have immediate relevancy to many police agencies that manage government grants and seized assets. One of them is concerned with the audit of federal law enforcement grants; the other of state police seized-asset revenues.

Audit of Law Enforcement Grant. Law enforcement agencies throughout the United States receive grants from the federal and state governments. The legislative and executive departments rely on audits of financial transactions and compliance with applicable laws and regulations to obtain information on how these grants are managed. Such audits serve as the basic control over whether public funds are spent as the legislature intended and to prevent loss of funds from fraud and abuse. The General Accounting Office (GAO) conducted this audit of the Law Enforcement Assistance Administration (LEAA)'s grant program (Comptroller General of the United States, 1980).

GAO auditors found that there were some serious issues related to the LEAA grant programs. Recipients at state and local levels were not being regularly audited and, where the recipients were audited, audit findings were not appropriately and quickly resolved. One of the issues was that grantees kept funds they were not entitled to under applicable laws and regulations. As a result, the government lost money that would otherwise have been collected or saved. A large number of audits remained unresolved because of delays in long transmittal time in forwarding audit reports to program managers responsible for resolving the audit findings and procrastination by program managers in acting on them. Inadequate audit resolution procedures and practices were found at some state planning agencies as well. Some state planning agency program managers did not review or resolve monetary findings; nor did they require that deficiencies be corrected before awarding subsequent grants.

GAO auditors recommended that the Attorney General direct the LEAA administrator to develop a coherent and comprehensive policy for achieving adequate audit coverage of all its grant recipients and launch an all-out effort to have all major grant recipients audited within the next two years in accordance with this policy. LEAA should issue guidelines for program managers to use in resolving audit findings and hold person or persons in program management responsible for timely and proper resolution of findings. It should designate an official independent of program management to monitor the substance of audit findings and the propriety of resolutions, and require that the official provide management with quarterly reports showing the disposition of audit findings. It should require that auditors track open findings until all recommended improvements were made, funds recovered, debts forgiven, or the findings determined to be in error. Written decisions should be required justifying why amounts shown to be due by the auditors' reports were not collected. Such decisions should be reviewed for legality and endorsed by the legal official who performed the review. The Attorney General should also direct LEAA's comptroller to provide positive accounting controls over collection of audit-related funds, and require that program managers and auditors systematically review the adequacy of state planning agency procedures and practices for issuing audit reports and resolving audit findings.

In response to these recommendations, the Department of Justice and LEAA indicated that they had been aware of the problems in LEAA's audit system and concurred in general with the GAO recommendations. The Department of Justice indicated that clearance of open audits was an administrative priority during the past year. The number of audits open after more than one year had been drastically reduced. Effort to clear audit reports was proceeding, and emphasis on newly issued audit reports was being maintained. LEAA was already taking actions to improve audit effectiveness in anticipation of the GAO recommendations. LEAA conducted studies of its program review function and of LEAA policy and procedures for clearance of audit reports. Its Management Advisory Task Force developed substantive criteria to guide the clearance of audit findings. LEAA had also set up an audit policy working group, which addressed implementation of government audit requirements, priorities for audit of compliance requirements, development of policy to assure consistent dispositions of audit findings, state planning agency roles during clearance of audits conducted by state and local audit agencies, opportunities to streamline clearance procedures, and establishment of policy for award of new grants to grantees with open audits.

LEAA reviewed the draft policy concerning audit requirements, which, based upon existing legislation and applicable federal government policies, provided for a more active agency role in assuring audit coverage recommended by GAO. LEAA developed draft criteria specifying when questioned costs must be sustained, when they could be allowed, when legal review or other expert advice was necessary, and when program managers should cut off or delay funding until recipients corrected the deficiencies identified by the auditors. LEAA's Audit Policy Working Group was assessing the adequacy of these criteria to identify gaps and develop recommendations in areas where additional guidance might be needed. The Department would require that all recipients have a financial/compliance audit on an organization-wide basis within two years. They would also require that grantees submit to LEAA an audit plan which would satisfy the requirements of the Office of Management and Budget Circular. Failure to comply with this condition was a substantial failure to comply with the provisions of the Omnibus Crime Control and Safe Streets Act and the regulations promulgated by the Administration. The grantee was on notice that such failure could result in suspension or termination of funding. Prior to receipt of the GAO draft report, LEAA had prepared a draft instruction to create an Audit Review Committee, which was responsible for ensuring the resolution and clearance of all audit reports not cleared within six months and making determinations on whether actions taken by the cognizant program office to clear a referred report were properly aggressive.

The Department of Justice did not fully concur with GAO's recommendation that program officials justify in writing uncollected amounts shown to be due in auditors' reports, and that such justifications be reviewed for legality and endorsed by a legal official. They proposed to develop new guidelines requiring discretion to be exercised by program managers. When the department officials considered their steps to establish policy together with their steps to assure review of their implementation, including formation of the Audit Review Committee, they believed that they had responded to the intent of this recommendation. Prior to the receipt of this report, LEAA had begun revising its instruction on collection of claims to institute the necessary controls. Once LEAA consolidated its directives affecting clearance of audit reports, program offices would keep the comptroller more effectively informed of amounts resolved, waived, excused, or to be collected.

Neither did the department believe that GAO considered the bases for clearance of findings, which could be discovered during resolution of a finding. It indicated that most questioned costs were not illegal but were only unsupported at the time of the audit. Through the clearance process, they could be appropriately cleared and justified without a dollar recovery. The department also had reservations about the implementation of the single audit concept stating that it would be difficult to audit all programs with one single guide and meet numerous unique legislative requirements established by Congress for federal programs. The department partially concurred with the recommendation that an independent official be required to provide management with quarterly reports showing the dispositions of audit findings, including the age and amounts of unresolved findings and results of the findings closed during the period. The system for tracking audit findings provided to management on a monthly basis much of the information called for by this recommendation. The tracking system was computerized and had the capability to report the aging of each report by cognizant program office, including the amount of questioned costs contained in each report.

Audit of State Police Seized Asset Revenues. Authorized through state and federal statutes, police departments forfeit millions of dollars of assets derived from or used in illegal activities every year. The proceeds from these forfeitures are often used to enhance law enforcement activities. Audits of police seized assets help the government obtain information about the revenues received by the police from asset forfeiture, expenditures from this source, and the ability of the police to project revenues. This audit, conducted by the State Legislative Commission on Expenditure Review (1991) examined the status of the Seized Asset Account of New York State Police, evaluated police methods for projecting revenues for budgeting, and identified spending patterns of this account.

The Legislative Commission on Expenditure Review (LCER) conducted an extensive file review to create a database to determine if the available data lent itself to reliable revenue projections. Two hundred twenty-five federal forfeiture cases initiated by the State Police between 1984 and 1990 were randomly sampled. This sample was representative of all cases with a confidence level of 90 percent and a 5 percent margin of error. Analysis of this sample, as well as data provided by the State Police and the Office of the State Comptroller provided the basis for the audit data. LCER staff also interviewed the state police officials and the State Division of Criminal Justice Services.

Most currency or property was seized by officers or investigators at the time of arrest or shortly thereafter. For larger cases, additional assets were uncovered with further investigation. Their file review showed that 79 percent of the value of seizures was currency, 11 percent personal property, and 10 percent real property. A single case might result in a number of items being seized. In their sample, cases had an average of 2.5 items. Forfeiture cases and any associated criminal cases were generally tried separately. Forfeiture cases could be prosecuted either civilly or criminally; however, most were decided civilly as the burden of proof was less stringent. Each item seized was prosecuted separately. Items could be prosecuted either judicially or administratively. Items valued at over $1 million, those contested, real property, and all customs cases were pursued judicially, while other cases were decided administratively. LCER's analysis showed that 86 percent of cases were administrative and 14 percent judicial. After the proceedings, the State Police and any other involved agencies were informed of the outcome through a forfeiture notice; and the check with their share was expected to follow shortly. The Federal Government determined the final share to be granted to involved agencies, based on the appeals process to this decision.

Between 1984 and 1991, the State Police were involved in seizures totaling over $153 million. Although a share of approximately $54 million was anticipated, $35 million of this remained outstanding as of January 1991. Forfeiture revenues were deposited in the Seized Asset Account established in 1986-87. The account received most of its revenues from forfeiture proceedings; about a half million dollars per year came from accident report and photograph fees, and the remainder were from other sources. Most asset forfeiture revenues collected over the five years before came to the state through the federal asset forfeiture process. This process was neither timely nor predictable. The State Police had taken steps to ensure that monies due were received in a reasonable time frame. This lag in collections had led the State Police to expend more from this account than they had collected. Over $42 million was expended, leaving a negative cash balance of over $17 million. Seized asset dollars were spent primarily on the State Police's investigation and patrol programs, with technical services receiving a sizable share over the past two years. Over the life of the account, expenditures were split almost evenly between personal and nonpersonal services.

The process for receiving money from the Federal Government, particularly in the early years, was lengthy averaging from two to three years with many cases still outstanding. As a result of several State Police initiatives, it appeared that this situation was improving. In projecting revenues the State Police did not have all available data.

However, a computer tracking system under development would allow easier access and manipulation of the necessary data. Still, the State Police needed to address the projection difficulties caused by the disproportionately large amount of dollars resulting from a very few cases. The State Police had not developed nor used a formal method for projecting revenues. Rather, they estimated collections based on the amount expected from currency cases "in the pipeline," that is, monies expected from federal forfeiture. In evaluating projections, LCER examined the degree of uncertainty between monies expected from the applications and monies actually received after the proceedings were completed. The time frame for receiving federally forfeited revenues was the most problematic aspect of projecting revenues. There was no consistency over time in the number of days it took for a case to be resolved and a check released to the state.

Given the unpredictable nature of seized asset revenues, the auditors examined expenditure trends to see if budgeting and spending patterns could be modified to limit the impact uncollectible revenues had on the State Police budget. The State Police's ability to project revenues would be improved with better use of available information. However, the problem of disproportionately large cases could hinder any projection technique. Although the State Police anticipated making use of expanded state laws, it was expected to have minimum impact on revenues and projections. The nature of drug activity and subsequent law enforcement and prosecution are likely to continue to cause forfeiture revenues to fluctuate from year to year regardless of how sophisticated projection techniques become.

The superintendent of New York State Police responded to the audit, pointing out that the first and foremost aim of the State Police was to investigate and identify drug dealers and make arrests, which would result in convictions and ultimately cripple the drug traffic within New York State. The agency concurred with the findings that the nature of drug activity and subsequent law enforcement and prosecution would likely continue to cause forfeiture revenues to fluctuate from year to year regardless of how sophisticated projections techniques became. The State Police had concentrated its efforts on ensuring that, once a seizure was completed, the shortest possible time elapsed before they received those funds.

Economy and Efficiency Audits

Economy and efficiency audits are evaluations that determine whether a police organization is acquiring, protecting, and using its resources economically and efficiently; the causes of uneconomical practices or inefficiencies; and whether the entity has complied with laws and regulations concerning matters of economy and efficiency. Economy and efficiency audits as applied to the police are often concerned with the use of human and material resources. The most important consideration is whether police officers have been deployed at the most economical and efficient level. Related to this are questions of staffing cost, police supervision, officer productivity, benefits and leave policy, and civilianization (National Audit Office, 1992a). Briefly described below are several cases of economy and efficiency audits, including audits of staffing and leave, police manpower, communication room, and fleet management.

Audit of Police Staffing and Leave. Police must make full use of human resources to increase efficiency due to the labor-intensive nature of police work. One way to use human resources efficiently is by developing and practicing a sound staffing and leave policy. Such policies and their practices are directly concerned with economy and efficiency of police operations and are thus important considerations of economy and efficiency audits. The audit of the New York City Transit Authority Police Department (TAPD) in 1991 was concerned with TAPD staffing and leave policies from 1988 to 1991 (Regan, 1991). The objectives of this audit were to determine whether the placement and retention of officers on restricted duty or no-work status because of injury or illness were justified; whether the unlimited sick leave policy was being abused; whether the police effectively deployed and supervised its patrol force; whether uniformed officers were performing jobs that could be better handled by civilians; and whether officers were adequately supervised while on patrol.

The auditors from the New York State Comptroller Office conducted this audit in accordance with generally accepted government auditing standards. They planned and performed the audit to assess those operations of the TAPD within their audit scope. They reviewed TAPD internal controls and compliance with those laws, rules, and regulations that were relevant to TAPD operations. The auditors' consideration of TAPD's internal control structure focused on administrative controls, which were related mainly to the authorization, assignment, and monitoring of officers on restricted duty and no-work assignments. They examined evidence supporting transactions recorded in the accounting and operating records and assessed the estimates, judgments, and decisions made by management. Their data collection involved a review of police policies, procedures, and records; interviews of police officials; and field observations. They also contacted other police departments to obtain comparative information and engaged independent medical experts to review a sample of police medical records.

Auditors reviewed various administrative assignments to determine why 27 percent of available TAPD officers were assigned thereto. They also reviewed several leave categories to ascertain if there were adequate controls over leave. They determined that the TAPD could return to full patrol duty about 287 uniformed officers who were inappropriately put on restricted duty or no-work status or who were performing administrative or clerical duties. From 1983 through 1990, the number of TAPD restricted duty assignments increased almost 400 percent. In 1990, an average of 334 officers or 9 percent of the police force were on restricted duty. A significant number of the officers on restricted duty and no-work status had remained in that status for many years. One cause of this problem was that the TAPD lacked a formal written policy setting forth the circumstances under which restricted duty or no-work status designations were to be made, how long officers should be allowed to remain in that status, and when disability retirement or termination provisions of the law should be invoked.

An independent medical peer-review organization reviewed a sample of the police medical records and found that in 45 percent of the cases reviewed, officers had been inappropriately placed on restricted duty or no-work status or there was insufficient documentation to validate the judgment of the TAPD's Medical Clinic. Their finding also indicated that TAPD did not sufficiently monitor the activities of officers on restricted duty and no-work status. In addition, they found that TAPD officers averaged 18.3 days of sick leave per year in 1989, which was more than double the amount of sick leave used by officers in other police departments. Of the 151 officers on no-work status, 58 percent continued to collect night differential pay premiums even though some had not worked for periods ranging up to 535 days.

They identified hundreds of positions filled by uniformed officers that could be civilianized at a lower cost. Some full-duty officers assigned to administrative jobs that did not require specialized skills could have been replaced by restricted duty officers. Where officers were placed on restricted duty, they were not assigned to districts that had the greatest need for clerical or administrative support. All the units reviewed could be staffed with either civilians or restricted duty officers or a combination of both, freeing up as many as 230 officers for patrol duty. In 1990, the TAPD recognized the need to civilianize and hired a consultant who identified more than 400 positions that could be civilianized. However, New York City budget constraints jeopardized hundreds of civilian positions requested by the TAPD and existing positions were cut.

The auditors recommended that the department establish written policies covering the circumstances under which an employee can be placed on restricted duty and the length of time officers can remain on restricted duty, file disability retirement papers for officers out of work for more than one year, reexamine the work assignments of all officers on permanent restricted duty, return to full duty all officers not medically required to be on restricted duty, reassign all officers on no-work status who can perform limited duty to restricted duty assignments, assign officers placed on restricted duty to the districts on the basis of district needs and where the officers can be most productively employed, identify full-duty officers who are performing administrative and clerical tasks that can be performed by restricted duty officers and reassign the full-duty officers to patrol duty, and continue efforts to obtain budget authority to accelerate the hiring of civilians to replace full-duty officers in administrative positions.

Because generous sick leave benefits can be abused, independent medical professionals should be hired to review the medical records and conduct physical examinations of all officers on restricted duty. If the review finds a high rate of inappropriate work status designations, consideration needs to be given to revamping the current system for making such designations. The department should review policies regarding paid leave, investigate the reasons for the unusually high number of sick days used by TAPD officers, consider revision of the unlimited sick leave benefit as an issue for future collective bargaining agreements, consider eliminating the night differential pay to officers on extended sick leave in future collective bargaining, and periodically monitor officers on no-work status to ensure that their status appropriately reflects their medical condition.

Audit of Police Manpower. Manpower represents the most significant proportion of police resources. The government providing the manpower clearly has an interest in how well manpower resources are being used. But a volatile set of measurement criteria for assessing the use of manpower is not easy to determine and does not lend itself readily to simple quantification because the nature of police work is diverse and complex and the need for manpower is often led by public expectations, by crime and accident rates, and by other factors that are often difficult to predict. The National Audit Office of the United Kingdom (1992b) conducted this audit of manpower use in Scotland. The objectives of this audit were to determine whether the Scottish Office Home and Health Department were able to ensure that manpower levels were commensurate with the needs of forces; how far the department succeeded in securing the civilianization of those police posts identified as suitable for civilianization; and how the department satisfied itself in the efficient use of police manpower resources.

Auditors from the National Audit Office examined documents and records of the Scottish Office Home and Health Department, which has departmental responsibility for the police in Scotland and the work of the chief inspector of constabulary and his staff. Since the chief constables were responsible for the efficient and effective use of resources, the National Audit Office invited and received from the chief constables of all Scottish police forces responses to a questionnaire. The auditors also held discussions with representatives of each force and accompanied inspectorate staff on visits to individual police forces. They were assisted in this audit and advised on police matters by a former chief constable and commissioner of the Metropolitan Police.

Auditors, on assessing manpower requirements, found that over the last decade seven of the eight Scottish forces increased their police establishments by between 5 and 26 percent, but the largest force had not increased its establishment. Police authorities, made up of committees of regional councils or joint boards, determined the number of police officers and civilians, set budgets for their police forces, and were responsible for providing the chief constable with resources necessary to police the area adequately and efficiently. Changes in manpower establishments, however, must be approved by the Secretary of State. The Department defined to police forces and police authorities the factors the Secretary of State considered in approving police manpower establishments. In making decisions on the payment of police grant or the approval of manpower levels, the Secretary of State and the Scottish Office relied upon the advice of Her Majesty's Inspectorate of Constabulary. The Inspectorate's decision on the merits of each case was based on professional judgment, its general knowledge of the force in question, the statistical information it had, and its discussions with the chief constable. But it was given little information on ways individual police officers spent their time or standards of performance they achieved and had to rely on its observations during inspection. It was difficult for the Inspectorate to reach a full assessment of police efficiency without an analysis of the use of existing manpower. Work was being undertaken by the Inspectorate to devise a formula to improve ways of assessing manpower establishments by relating force manpower to characteristics of the police area. The formula may provide a means of assessing the relative needs of the eight forces in Scotland, but more information related to specific force objectives is required.

On civilianization, auditors found that although forces had identified further posts for civilianization, there had nevertheless been considerable increases in police manpower approved since 1986. Until recently, the Scottish Office Department and the Inspectorate had inadequate information on progress in civilianizing posts and there was no record of the number of police officers released to operational duties as a result of civilianization. An average of 66 percent of posts suitable for civilianization were filled by civilians in Scotland by 1990. Progress in civilianizing posts depended on the enthusiasm of chief constables and on the support of police authorities to fund the civilian costs. The auditors estimated that some 2,040 posts could be civilianized in Scotland. If progress in civilianization had been faster and a larger number of police officers had been released for operational duties, some of the increases of Scottish police officers might have been unnecessary. The Scottish Department calculated that the national annual saving arising from civilianization was £14,000 for each officer. The auditors noted, therefore, that savings could have been achieved if better progress had been made in civilianization; and that with 500 posts remaining to be civilianized and assuming the 88 percent target, savings of some £7 million a year could in principle be achieved in the future.

On how the Scottish Department satisfied itself in police efficiency, the Department accepted that the assessment of efficiency would be greatly assisted if forces provided the Inspectorate with an activity analysis of how police time was spent. All Inspectorate reports did not define the criteria against which efficiency was judged nor had the Inspectorate reported on the relative efficiencies of individual forces. The Inspectorate recognized the difficulties in assessing police efficiency and developed a matrix of indicators for Scotland, which allowed data on Scottish forces to be compared with data from other United Kingdom forces. The Secretary of State had statutory power to withhold police grant if he was not satisfied with a force's efficiency. The Department recognized that improvements in assessing police performance were needed and could be achieved.

The auditors from the National Audit Office believe that the Inspectorate occupied a unique and influential position in relationship to the police service and should fully exploit its role by providing police forces with sufficient feedback on how well they operated. The rapid development of more systematic and objective assessment of police efficiency should be actively encouraged to aid the Inspectorate's work. In the interests of economy and efficiency, the Scottish Department should ensure that consent to increases in uniformed manpower is only given if it is clear that civilianization opportunities have been utilized and put into effect as far as practicable.

Audit of Police Communication Rooms. Effective communication is a core requirement for building successful businesses and a crucial aspect of policing (Hargie & Tourish, 2009; Kim & Mauborgne, 2003). Police communications are also an important operational matter, with major resource implications. Because of the central role of communication rooms in the resource allocation process, the Audit Commission (1990) reviewed their structure and operation as part of its program of work in fifteen provincial police forces in England and Wales. Conducted at a time when the systems which underpinned police communications were undergoing rapid changes in technology, this audit was aimed at determining whether forces had established standards of service for the communication rooms, how communication room operations were evaluated, and whether police resources could be saved through restructuring of police communication rooms.

The Audit Commission found that few forces specified the standards of service they expected. Fewer still monitored their actual performance. Most forces did not know how long operators took to answer calls from the public or the delay before patrol officers arrived at incidents. Communications room operators implemented force policy on the type of officers to send to incidents and the degree of urgency. The audit findings indicated that many forces could improve both the quality and the efficiency of their service. Forces should monitor closely the key aspects of their performance, particularly the time taken to answer calls, the quality of the advice given, and the time taken for officers to reach the incident. There was potential to reduce costs by around 15 percent based on analysis of data from the forces studied.

The Audit Commission suggested that the reduction of running cost could be achieved by making more efficient use of staff and increasing the use of civilians. Forces should use staff more efficiently by seeking economies of scale. Efficiency increases sharply as the number of operators in the room increases to four, more gradually thereafter. Forces should therefore avoid communications rooms which do not have sufficient workload to require at least four operators to be on duty for the majority of the day. Forces should use more flexible shift systems. One large communication room, for example, can match staffing levels to variations in workload over the 24-hour period, thereby saving £500,000 over a traditional four shift system. They should also provide suitable support systems such as modern telephone networks and information technology.

The Audit Commission recommended that all forces review the performance of their communications service without delay. They should set standards for the time taken to answer calls and dispatch resources and for call grading, then monitor time taken to answer calls and dispatch resources against standards, and monitor how calls were graded statistically and qualitatively. If the force is not efficient, they should review communications structure, including size of rooms, staffing, support systems, shift systems, and civilianization policy. Forces should also conduct periodic surveys of operational officers to obtain their views about the service provided by the communications rooms.

Audit of Fleet Management. Another major police operational area where running cost could be reduced is fleet management. The Audit Commission (1992) examined the fleet management in many police forces in Britain. It found that after employees, transport was the largest item of police expenditure, typically accounting for approximately 20 percent of nonstaff-related costs. The five main issues addressed by the audit were management arrangement, fleet utilization, fleet management functions, vehicle maintenance, and fuel. Compared with other public sector fleets, police vehicles are unusual in the sense that their annual mileage is high. This led to a high fleet turnover rate, more frequent servicing, and fuel accounting for a relatively high proportion of total cost.

A critical issue was how much day-to-day involvement police officers should have with vehicle management. The Audit Commission's view was that officers were less likely than civilian managers to have the necessary expertise to manage fleets economically and efficiently. The role of police officers should be restricted to their duties as the "client" for the transport. Auditors' fieldwork at five forces together with their previous knowledge of police fleet operations suggested that the areas offering greatest scope for improvement were vehicle utilization and vehicle maintenance.

The auditors found that fleet mix and the number of vehicles allocated to each division and squad were rarely reviewed by forces despite changes in methods of policing. More effort was required to identify the real needs of transport users. An untapped source of utilization data was in vehicle log books, which could help in matching supply to demand. Some forces' vehicle workshop practices needed to be overhauled by eliminating overstaffing, reviewing traditional work-content bonus schemes, and reducing the frequency with which vehicles underwent routine services. All forces, especially rural ones, needed to review the location of their workshops and their willingness to use private garages or local authority workshops in areas where a police workshop could not be justified.

The Audit Commission recommended that responsibilities for fleet management be clearly defined; fleet management be undertaken by a specialist, wholly civilianized section; and nonmaintenance staff there be reduced. The transport section should be a self-standing cost center with its own trading account. The full costs of operating should be identified correctly; consideration should be given to collaborating with a local authority transport department. And there should be an adequate computerized fleet management system. The fleet size should be relative to the number of officers below average, taking account of the density of population. The fleet mix should be in line with the guidelines. The allocation of the fleet between users should be determined by objective criteria. The vehicle allocation ratios should be in line with the good practice indictors. The fleet utilization should meet the target indicators.

Specific recommendations were made for fleet management functions, repairs and maintenance, and fuel. For fleet management functions, the transport manager should consult with users about the specification of new vehicles; the proportion of the fleet should be accounted for by two manufacturers; and certain level of discount should be generally achieved on new vehicles. The transport manager should have sufficient powers to adopt cost-effective procurement strategies. Auctions should be used for disposing of vehicles. And the merits of different types of insurance policies should be investigated. For repairs and maintenance, the full costs of running the workshop should be identified. An hourly rate should be calculated for fitters based on productive hours. The costs of repairs and maintenance should not be recharged to individual vehicles using an hourly rate. The fleet management should have information about the repair and maintenance cost, the interval between scheduled visits to the workshop, and the costs of ferrying vehicles from base to workshops. The force should consider using either private garages or local authority workshops for some maintenance work and consider a traditional work-content based bonus scheme. For fuel, fleet management should have accurate data on the fuel consumption of individual vehicles, monitor and act upon this data, give total mileage limits to users, and consider the merits of diesel vehicles.

Program Results and Effectiveness Audits

Police audits concerning program results and effectiveness determine the extent to which desired results or benefits established by the legislature or other authorizing body are achieved and the effectiveness of organizations, programs, activities, or functions in reaching their goals and objectives (General Accounting Office, 1994). Various police programs have been audited in terms of their results and effectiveness, depending on how desired results and effectiveness are defined. If a state police program's objective is to provide adequate security for selected state-owned or leased buildings, the accomplishment of such security as perceived by most state employees working in those buildings would be considered a measure of effectiveness (Legislative Division of Post Audit, 1993). If a police program's objective is to complete the implementation of a radio system, the successful installation of such a system would be deemed the result of the program (Lester, 1993). The audits described in the following are concerned with program results and effectiveness of police training, police communication, team policing, police community partnership, child recovery, and fingerprint service.

Audit of Local Police Training Program. Maintaining a sufficient number of high-quality police training programs in a state is necessary for effective law enforcement, greater productivity, and protection against lawsuits. This audit conducted by the Legislative Commission on Expenditure Review (LCER) (1986) assessed the adequacy of the number and quality of local police and peace officer training programs in the State of New York and the State's monitoring and technical assistance roles. The 1959 Police Officer Legislation established a predominantly locally organized and financed police training structure with the state responsible for monitoring and providing technical assistance. The Municipal Police Training Council was responsible for implementing the statutory mandates. The Council granted New York City police officers the exemptions allowed under the statute. The Bureau for Municipal Police (BMP) in the State Division of Criminal Justice Services was the staff unit for the Council.

Auditors from the Legislative Commission on Expenditure Review (LCER) reviewed files to assess BMP monitoring of training programs and instructors, compared 1985 basic training courses with the new 400-hour course mandate, assessed the statewide evenness of training, and reviewed compliance with training mandates. Samples of officers were selected from BMP's computer data base to measure compliance with mandatory recruit and supervisory training. All chiefs and sheriffs and graduates of recent basic training programs were surveyed on the sufficiency and quality of training provided. To supplement the surveys, LCER staff interviewed training zone coordinators in 9 of the

12 training zones outside New York City to assess the quality and sufficiency of training available. Almost 60 percent of the trainees and nearly 80 percent of the chiefs and sheriffs surveyed responded to the LCER surveys. New York State's mandated police training programs were compared to training provided by the New York State Police, the New York City Police Department, and other states and national police training standards.

The auditors found that all mandated and nonmandated police training was organized locally through the 13 training zones. The BMP staff provided most of the highway safety and crime prevention courses covering breathalyzer, radar, crash management, crime prevention, and related subjects. BMP had four units which were directly involved in monitoring or providing police and peace officer training. BMP's professional staff had risen from 41 in 1980-81 to 50 in 1985-86 with the greatest rises over the past two years. BMP State Purposes expenditures rose from $598,040 in 1980-81 to $1,895,353 in 1985-86, an increase of 217 percent.

Chiefs and sheriffs in each zone determined the need for a basic school. The largest departments assumed most of the basic school costs including facilities and instructors. Beyond providing an occasional instructor, BMP assistance for the basic training school was primarily limited to canvassing for recruits when requested to do so and providing law books in three subject areas. Slightly under 90 percent of the recruits completed basic training within the mandated one year. Over two-thirds of the sample finished the basic course within six months. However, slightly under one-third of the recruits from small departments—those with 25 or fewer officers—did not meet the one year mandate. Recruits from small departments also more frequently reported being assigned to one-officer patrol and carrying firearms before formal training than officers from medium or large-size departments. Officers attending a part-time basic school also were less likely to meet the one year mandate and more apt to indicate they were on one-officer patrol or were issued firearms before training. There was an uneven distribution of part-time basic schools. The six zones with the fewest or no part-time basic courses all had a greater proportion of part-time officers than the statewide average excluding New York City and were largely rural. As a result, part-time officers were less likely to complete the basic course within the one year mandate.

Of sergeants outside New York City born after 1948, 91.8 percent had completed the course; 6.9 percent had not finished the course; and 1.3 percent were deputy sheriffs who were exempt from the mandate. Almost half of the training zone coordinators indicated that the six-month period for completion of the police supervision course was generally not met; about one-third believed that the mandate was being met with minor exceptions; and the rest felt it was routinely met or had no opinion. Almost three-quarters of the chiefs and sheriffs were satisfied with the number of police supervision schools available in their area.

Enforcement of compliance with the training mandates rested with local civil service commissions. BMP's role in promoting compliance was notifying the State Civil Service Commission of officers completing mandated courses. Over the past two years, BMP monitoring of basic schools consisted largely of a paper review of curricula. BMP monitoring of peace officer training programs had also been limited principally to a paper review of compliance with Municipal Police Training Council regulations.

Slightly over 90 percent of the basic recruit graduates rated their training as either useful or extremely useful. Firearms training, field training, arrest techniques, and justified use of force received the highest rating. Almost 90 percent of the chiefs and sheriffs surveyed felt that the base course was extremely useful or useful in preparing officers for their initial assignments. Instruction in firearms training, justified use of force, and arrest techniques had the highest proportion of excellent ratings by recruits. No subject area had a combined excellent and good rating of less than 65 percent. Over 90 percent of the chiefs and sheriffs expressed satisfaction with the basic school instruction. Firing ranges received the most positive assessment of the basic course facilities and equipment used with 86.3 percent good or excellent responses. Outdoor facilities garnered the lowest positive rating of 62.5 percent. The largest proportion of recruits wanted increased training in field training, criminal investigation, and arrest techniques. Trainees expressed the desire to have more practical training geared to their day-to-day responsibilities including hands-on emergency vehicle operation, street survival tactics, court testimony and paperwork, and physical training.

Almost all of the chiefs and sheriffs were satisfied with the instruction and content of BMP courses. Over 90 percent felt that BMP had satisfactorily publicized its own courses, while over four-fifths indicated that the bureau had adequately publicized other training programs. The New York City and the New York State Police training programs significantly exceeded the Municipal Police Training mandates. Their basic courses had substantially more hours in firearms and field training. They also provided at least 200 hours of physical training where BMP had no mandate to do so. Only six of the 35 basic courses held in 1985 met a national standard of 160 hours of field training.

The auditors concluded that the regional cooperative system failed to provide adequate training in several areas. A significant proportion of small departments and departments with part-time officers were assigning recruits to one-officer patrol or issuing them firearms prior to formal training. Some local departments might be vulnerable, therefore, to lawsuits based upon allegations of inadequate training. Although BMP had begun to rectify its past minimal monitoring of training schools, instructors, and curricula, it still needed to formulate solutions for the few weaknesses in the regional training structure. The auditors recommended that BMP develop a system to notify local civil service commissions and local police departments of officers who need the mandated basic and police supervision courses and address the lack of basic courses available for part-time police officers in some areas of the State. BMP should survey local departments to determine the current level of in-service training, make recommendations to the Municipal Police Training Council on the amount and type of required in-service training, and develop standardized tests for all recruits to ensure that officers have adequate knowledge of the basic course curriculum. The legislature needs to consider requiring that deputy sheriffs performing law enforcement functions complete the basic and police supervision training courses required of other police officers, prohibiting local law enforcement agencies and employers of peace officers from issuing firearms to officers who have not completed the basic training on firearms and justified use of force, and prohibiting local law enforcement agencies from assigning officers to one-officer patrol prior to completion of the basic training course except specified emergency circumstances.

In response to these recommendations, BMP officials indicated that it was generally a fair appraisal of the past and current status of local police training in New York State. However, there were areas within the report that warrant explanation and in some instances the inclusion of additional information for the purpose of clarification. They suggested that BMP, within the Division of Criminal Justice Services, was the staff arm of the Municipal Police Training Council. BMP was not in a position to impose standards on the police community, but rather to make recommendations, which were then submitted to the Municipal Police Training Council (MPTC) for their action. Any new mandates or changes to existing ones were within the purview of the MPTC. With regard to the basic course for police officers, BMP was responsible for the course from start to finish. BMP officials also pointed out that standards of the Commission on Accreditation for Law Enforcement Agencies should not be quoted as the standards against which to judge any aspect of police training. Statewide mandated programs had to be more flexible to meet the needs of many different agencies. They were considering how the State might support a centralized local police academy. Their response addressed also the issues of part-time schools, the drop in the number of crime prevention courses, insufficient monitoring of peace officer training, the need for a comprehensive examination process for recruit training, and instructor certifications for police training.

Audit of Team Policing Program. In the 1970s, many police departments in the United States implemented team policing programs, where teams of patrol officers and detectives worked collaboratively and took joint responsibility for serving relatively confined areas with traditional neighborhood boundaries. This audit of the team policing program and its effect on clearance rate was conducted at Rochester, New York, Police Department at a time when Rochester police were organizing neighborhood teams of officers and detectives in an effort to control crime (Block & Ulberg, 1974). The purpose of the audit was to determine whether the team policing program had contributed to improvements in the targeted areas.

Four data sources were examined for this study. The first was the computer records of offenses and police disposition for eight areas before and after introduction of the team concept. Comparison areas were selected by dividing each of three police units into parts. Unit A contained Team A and Comparison A. Unit B included Team B and Comparison B1 and B2. Unit C covered Team C and comparison C1 and C2. Data on offenses of robbery, burglary, larceny and criminal trespass for each of these eight areas were gathered for one year before the introduction of the teams and one year after.

The second data source was computer records of arrests by officers on the teams and officers in a comparison group not assigned to the teams. The number of arrests made by each of the officers in the teams in the before and during periods was compared with the number of arrests made by comparison group officers. Comparison officers were selected by using the IBM numbers assigned to each officer in the department. Each team officer was matched with the officer who had the next highest IBM number and who was in the same unit (but not on a team) in the during period. Some team and comparison officers selected were not members of the police department before the introduction of the teams. These officers were dropped from the sample, causing the number of Team C and Comparison C officers and investigators to be different.

The third data source consisted of all the dispatch assignment cards (4000) and reports (1200) filed during six selected days, half of which occurred before and half during the use of teams. The same day of the week and month was chosen for each of the three days in the before and during periods. Information was collected on the nature of the offense, the reclassification, the officers involved, and whether or not there was an arrest.

The fourth data source was a computer printout of offenses cleared by arrest during two three-month periods: one period before and one period during the use of teams. For each of the approximately 1200 offenses cleared by arrest during these periods, the arrest report was checked to find the name of the arrested person. If the computer printout was verified by finding an arrest, the person's arrest folder was checked to determine the disposition of the case.

The audit found that reported differences cannot be accounted for by differences present when the teams were introduced. So higher clearance rates did not exist in team areas before the introduction of teams. Team officers made more arrests than officers in comparison areas. There was a slight tendency for teams to have a higher percentage of junior officers, but this was not statistically significant. Neither the teams themselves nor the Central Records Division significantly reclassified crimes downward in team areas. There were no arrest quality differences between the teams and the rest of the city. Correction of mistakes in computer records would have further increased clearance rates in the team areas. Increases in clearance and arrest rates were significant in themselves. They became even more significant if followed by a corresponding decrease in the crime rate. Crime rates went down more in the team areas than in the comparison areas. Especially notable was the drop in burglaries in the Team C area, a dramatic decrease compared to the comparison areas. The teams looked significantly better when crime rates in their areas were compared to the rest of the city.

As a result of the analysis, this audit concluded that the Rochester police statistics did hold up and suggested plans for a more intensive study to determine how the team program had affected investigations in the Rochester department. The Rochester department believed its success could be attributed to improvements in preliminary and follow-up investigations. There were also other possible explanations such as improved patrol supervision, reduced response times to crime calls, increased community relations due to the team effort, and better understanding of crime patterns due to a stronger emphasis on neighborhood protection. A more intensive study seemed appropriate for determining the process by which improvements had occurred. Certain findings of this study were particularly indicative of the importance of the Rochester team policing program and of the value of the investigative processes used by the teams. Robbery, burglary and larceny arrests should be studied to determine whether it was the investigative techniques that were responsible for the increased arrests.

Audit of the Police-Community Partnership. There needs to be more positive involvement of the police, the local community, and various agencies concerned in the design and execution of policing and partnership initiatives. Working together would make a significant contribution to the success of police-community partnership programs. Although this understanding is commonly shared by the police and the community, specific approaches to building an effective partnership and measuring its effectiveness have not been fully developed. In this audit, the National Audit Office (1992c) examined approaches used by five inner-city divisions in London (i.e., Brixton, Hackney, Lewisham, Stoke Newington, and Tottenham) for reducing crime. These five divisions were chosen because of their comparability with one another.

The National Audit Office visited Metropolitan Police Head-quarters, four of the eight areas, and the five selected divisions. The auditors sought the views of the police and community consultative groups and held meetings with the divisions and groups. They also consulted the Home Office and the chairman of the independent working group on the Local Delivery of Crime Prevention through the Partnership Approach and Crime Concern. A chief superintendent from the Metropolitan Police was seconded as a member of the investigating team to help the auditors with their inquiries and provided professional advice during the fieldwork. The National Audit Office reviewed the application of the partnership approach in practice in the selected divisions; the planning, management, and delivery of police tasks; the information and analysis available on crime and police activity; the general problems of measuring police performance in tackling crime; and the assessment of performance in the selected divisions. Because it is important that divisions respond to local problems and needs in ways they consider most appropriate, the auditors assessed performance against the targets the divisions set for themselves, using their own measures and a package of indicators developed by the National Audit Office for this study at the request of the Metropolitan Police.

The auditors found that about 25 percent of police time was spent on crime-related work. On the partnership approach to crime reduction, the Metropolitan Police had done much to promote the concept of partnership, but more could be done in practice in the five divisions to realize the potential benefits. There were problems in monitoring and evaluating partnership activity partly because many initiatives were still in an early stage of development and results had not started to come through. But divisions could have done a better job in keeping adequate records of their activity and results achieved.

In examining the five divisions' assessment of their performance in tackling crime in 1990–91, the audit found that none of the divisions quantified the targets they set themselves. Each division sought to assess its performance against aims and objectives determined at the beginning of the year. This sometimes proved impossible as the way objectives were expressed made subsequent evaluations very difficult. The criteria used to assess performance varied from division to division and often from year to year. In assessing performance, the divisions took account of external circumstances and the impact of other work, including the need to respond to serious crimes. Some assessments were made of the effect of staffing changes on a division's work, but these were not normally linked to performance in specific priority areas.

The National Audit Office's reevaluation of divisional performance provided additional information and analysis on the results achieved, pointing to areas that divisions would need to examine to establish the reasons for success or failure. Had more information been available, this kind of analysis could have been extended for all the divisions to link arrests and clear-ups with those crimes selected for priority investigation. This would have enabled the divisions to know more about the relative effectiveness of prevention and detection, to identify the level of resources devoted to particular initiatives, and to determine whether the methods chosen represented a cost-effective and efficient response to the problems identified. This would also have enabled divisions to decide whether similar initiatives should be undertaken in the future. The National Audit Office was unable to reevaluate many of the initiatives undertaken by the divisions, whose assessments varied widely in scope and depth. The information needed to assess an initiative frequently had either not been identified or not been retained.

The National Audit Office provided recommendations in several areas. On planning, management, and delivery, it recommended that divisions develop their current planning methods to improve the identification of priorities and ensure that these take proper account of both police and community needs. The divisions should relate their action plans more expressly to their declared aims, including the scope, opportunities, and difficulties of partnership. The monitoring of action plans and initiatives should be improved. The Coordinating and Task Groups in each division should focus more on decision-making and monitoring and assessing the progress of work, results achieved, and lessons learned.

On crime information and analysis, it recommended that the five divisions extend and improve crime analysis to make a greater contribution to planning and operations and the assessment of results. The Metropolitan Police should consider the scope for making more use of crime analysis in the planning and execution of divisional crime reduction work as a full-time job for good quality staff with appropriate training. Further steps are needed to improve the planning, monitoring, analysis, and evaluation of police work so that greater benefit and impact are obtained from available resources. As the Metropolitan Police moves forward with the partnership approach and develops new approaches to its work such as sector policing, it will become even more important to identify what has worked well and what has not.

On measuring police performance, the auditors believed that the performance indicator package developed by the National Audit Office in consultation with the Metropolitan Police Service would enable a more well-rounded assessment to be made of a division's performance. The National Audit Office's selected yardsticks would be helpful for comparing output figures against current targets, previous performance, and results of similar divisions; assessing a division's achievements as a whole taking into account manpower, costs, and public opinion as well as crime figures; identifying important trends over time such as the level of allegations and percentage of crimes solved; developing relevant performance standards that reflect the division's particular circumstances and policing style; and identifying areas of common interest and concern to similar divisions. The package of indicators can be used to profile a division's achievements under the main headings of crime, operations, resources, and quality of service. It can also be used to analyze a division's impact on crime. For this purpose, the indicators would show level of crime, measure of its seriousness and solvability, link between arrests and clear-ups, division's response to crime recorded and crime screened in, how police have been used in relation to arrests, clear-ups, and initiatives, how divisional money has been spent, and fear of crime and public satisfaction. The performance indicators can also be used to evaluate a particular divisional initiative.

Audit of Child Recovery Programs. State police agencies are usually charged with the responsibility to recover missing children and prevent them from being victimized by abductors, molesters, or exploiters. Office of the Auditor General of the State of Illinois (Templeman, 1992) conducted this audit of the state police child recovery program (called I SEARCH in Illinois) at the direction of the Illinois Legislative Audit Commission. The purpose of the audit was to determine the amount of funds expended on the child search program, its mission, activities, and accomplishments, and whether measures used by the police to assess program effectiveness were appropriate. The audit was conducted in accordance with the generally accepted government auditing standards, the audit standards promulgated by the Illinois State Office of the Auditor General, and the Illinois State Auditing Act.

The auditors interviewed officials responsible for the child search program from the State Police Divisions of Criminal Investigation, Administration, and State Troopers. They contacted officials at the State Departments of Alcoholism and Substance Abuse, Children and Family Services, State Board of Education, Federal Department of Justice, Office of Juvenile Justice and Delinquency Prevention, National Center for Missing and Exploited Children, National Fingerprint Program for Child Identification, and Federal Bureau of Investigation. They also contacted officials in 11 states to determine how programs similar to the Illinois child search program are evaluated. In addition, they contacted three academicians experienced in juvenile issues concerning appropriate criteria for measuring program effectiveness. They reviewed statutes, administrative rules, and State Police policies and procedures related to the child search program, and assessed the adequacy of the State Police's internal controls over the administration of the program and accuracy of data. They examined data from the Comptroller's Office and State Police on the appropriations and expenditures for the child search and related programs. They surveyed all 52 employees identified on the child search program payroll as of June 1991 to determine the amount of working time spent on the program. They examined the records of grants awarded by the State Police to local child search units for each year since 1985. Using the amounts awarded for fiscal year 1990, they selected and visited 10 sites, reviewed records and documents at each local unit visited, and sampled closed cases from 1990 and cases open at the time of their visit.

The auditors found that most children reported missing were runaways who returned home within a few days. Overall, 99 percent of the 39,587 cases reported in fiscal year 1990 were cleared. Of the 52 state police employees paid from the program funds in fiscal year 1991, only seven reported working full time on child search activities. The number of local units awarded child search grant funds decreased from 87 to 22 since 1988. From fiscal year 1985 through 1991, the child search expenditures totaled about $26 million, an average of about $3.7 million a year. A separate child search appropriation was discontinued in fiscal year 1992. Child search accomplishments included establishing an information clearinghouse, expanding a statewide computerized reporting system for missing children, delivering training and disseminating information to local police officials, establishing a missing children hotline, and allocating grant funds to local units to conduct child search activities.

A fundamental problem was found concerning the accuracy of data reported to the State Police by local agencies. Local police agencies often inaccurately reported classification categories, recovery activities, and other data to the State Police. Some local agencies were not timely in reporting missing children. As a result of these problems, complete information on missing children in Illinois was not available. Until reporting problems are corrected, the extent of the problem with missing children cannot be accurately portrayed. Additionally, data had not been maintained in a way that would allow an assessment of program effectiveness. If complete and accurate missing child information was collected, the State Police could begin designing measures of effectiveness. These measures could include an analysis of changes over time in the number of cases in the entire state and between geographic regions and follow-up studies on awareness of child search information.

While no formal evaluations or studies of program effectiveness had been done, State Police officials stated that they assessed the child search programs by using the percentage of cases that had been cleared. The percentage of cases cleared, however, was not an accurate indicator of effectiveness according to other state and national officials. The number of recoveries or cases where police were physically involved in returning the child would be more significant and useful in trend analysis and resource planning although it would still be only an indirect measure of effectiveness. State Police officials also measured whether the goals and objectives stated in the local unit grant applications were met and whether grant money was spent effectively by the local units and as authorized by the State Police. While these measures are reasonable, State Police reviews of the local units were financial-related and did not measure effectiveness. The measure on whether there was a high level of public awareness and receptiveness to the local unit activities, another indicator used by the state, was theoretically sound as an indicator of the program's effectiveness, but was difficult to assess without repeated attitudinal surveys.

The auditors recommended that the Director of the State Police require that complete and accurate information on missing children be entered into the Law Enforcement Agency Data System (LEADS). All local police agencies should enter correct data, including proper care classification codes and four-letter cancellation codes. If the Director is unable to obtain compliance from local law enforcement agencies, he should seek enhanced statutory authority from the General Assembly. The Director should comply with the Intergovernmental Missing Child Recovery Act and ensure that the child search annual report is produced, including the appropriation for the previous fiscal year indicating the grant amount each child search unit received. The Director should also ensure that the local units report in the quarterly reports only those recoveries the police were directly involved in or where police investigative efforts were responsible for determining the child's whereabouts. Local law enforcement agencies involved with the search should enter all information related to missing and runaway children into the LEADS as soon as possible.

The State Police officials concurred with the recommendations and indicated that they had been striving for complete and accurate information for all data entered into the LEADS. They will continue to monitor closely local agencies to ensure compliance with state guidelines. While the expanded cancellation codes are optional fields, their use and importance will be stressed in the department's continual training program. In light of reduced funding for the child search units, they suggested a separate annual report and asked for necessary legislative changes. They will make every effort to ensure that only those children physically recovered by local police or another agency through involvement of the child search unit are counted. They will continue to advise all law enforcement agencies in Illinois on the requirement that a report of a missing child be entered into LEADS as soon as a minimal level of data is obtained. This will be accomplished through training, informational bulletins, and periodic LEADS messages.

Audit of Fingerprint Service. Fingerprint service is a small but important part of police operations. It accounts for less than 1 percent of police expenditure but offers a unique system of crime detection because it helps identify offenders as well as provide evidence to secure convictions. From this perspective, the audit of fingerprint service should be considered an effectiveness rather than an efficiency audit. The Audit Commission in the United Kingdom (1992) conducted this audit of fingerprint services in provincial police forces in England and Wales at a time when most of these police forces were operating significantly below their potential in terms of number of identifications obtained from fingerprints left at crime scenes. In 1987, these forces recorded over two million crimes, including burglaries and motor vehicle thefts, where fingerprints might have been left. Yet only 40,000 or less than 2 percent of offenders were identified using fingerprints.

The Audit Commission found that this situation existed because in many forces resources for fingerprint service were used either ineffectively or insufficiently. There was a very wide variation in performance between fingerprint bureaus–some bureaus obtained six times as many identifications per fingerprint officer as others. There was a serious imbalance between resources applied to collecting prints from scenes and those applied to comparing prints against collections. Overall, forces' ability to collect prints significantly outstripped their ability to search them thoroughly. Of the two million crimes referred to above, only one in three were examined for fingerprints and in some forces less than 10 percent of the prints submitted were searched.

This finding indicates that a large number of offenders who could have been identified by the fingerprint service were not apprehended and might go on to commit further offenses. The auditors estimated that if efficiently and adequately funded, the fingerprint service should be able to achieve two and a half times its existing number of identifications–an extra 60,000 identifications a year. In the medium term, the introduction of new technology providing a high speed, computerized automatic fingerprint recognition and retrieval system may revolutionize the fingerprint service. Meanwhile, there is much room for improving the organization and management of the service. In addition, the auditors found that morale was a key issue as work in the fingerprint service could be monotonous and staff was often poorly paid. In some forces, those working for the fingerprint service felt alienated from the remainder of the force. Unless the issue of motivation is addressed, there is little prospect of a significant improvement in performance.

The Audit Commission recommended that a diagnostic model be used for evaluating the effectiveness of each force's service and made a number of practical suggestions for improving the management of the service and increasing its effectiveness in detecting crime. For assessing performance, future auditors should determine opportunities for improvement as highlighted in the diagnostic model, differences in workload and quality of service in different parts of the force area in large forces, effective cost per identification offers best value for money for forces using a regional bureau, and a clear policy on the distribution of work for forces using both a regional and in-house bureau.

To improve performance, the Audit Commission recommended that forces determine standards for activities in several different areas. For activities at the scene, they should obtain information on how the force decides which crime scenes are to be visited by crime scene officers, whether the allocation of crime scene officers' resources reflect workload, whether there is a case for allowing crime scene officers to use private transport, and whether crime scene officers respond promptly to offenses reported. For fingerprinting of persons arrested, charged, or cautioned, forces should determine whether force general orders on fingerprinting accurately reflect the powers incorporated in Police and Criminal Evidence Act 1984 (PACE), whether the force fingerprint collection is updated promptly, and whether there is any evidence that the quality of fingerprints taken may be a cause for concern.

For maintaining fingerprint collections, forces should weed the search collections regularly and subdivide them geographically. For search procedures, forces should ensure that the level of suspect-checking is reasonable, elimination prints are obtained in all instances requested, prints recovered from crime scenes are searched promptly and thoroughly, and resources available to search prints are adequate and realistic in relation to number of crime scenes officers employed. The force's ability to collect prints should be balanced by its ability to search them with appropriate degree of thoroughness. For management and motivation, forces should monitor individual performance, take initiatives to enhance job satisfaction, provide adequate clerical support, and create opportunities for civilianization. For new technology, forces should consider purchasing automatic filing and retrieval equipment for their fingerprint bureaus.

Efficiency and Effectiveness Audits Combined

Performance audits oftentimes put equal emphasis on reviewing efficiency and effectiveness of police programs. The audit of the Criminal Investigation Bureau in the following is such an audit as it focuses on both administrative efficiency and operational effectiveness in criminal investigation. Another audit introduced in this section, the audit of financial management in police forces in the United Kingdom, is also such an audit because it is concerned with alignment of financial management efficiency with operational effectiveness. The last audit described in this section is a review of police answers to calls for service, which takes into account both the economy of police responses to calls and public satisfaction in contacting the police.

Audit of Criminal Investigations Bureau. The Arizona Office of the Auditor General conducted this audit of the Criminal Investigations Bureau of the Arizona Department of Public Safety pursuant to a resolution of the Joint Legislative Oversight Committee of Arizona State (Norton, 1992). The purpose was to obtain detailed information about the cases investigated by the Criminal Investigations Bureau (CIB), analyze the efficiency of case processing, and compare the quality and success of the Bureau to other law enforcement agencies presenting similar cases to the same prosecutorial agency.

The methods used include interviews, review of case files, and observations of Criminal Investigations Bureau (CIB) activities. The auditors analyzed the outcomes of three years' criminal cases presented for prosecution to the Maricopa and Pima County Attorneys' Offices. In Maricopa County, they examined the percentage of cases submitted that were filed for prosecution, the percentage of cases submitted of which attorneys requested further investigation by the enforcement agency, and the frequency with which the enforcement agency responded to the prosecutor's requests. They also examined other factors such as conviction rates, filing rates at the charge level, case characteristics, and dismissal reasons. In Pima County, they examined the percentage of cases filed by attorneys but dismissed prior to indictment and the percentage of defendants that were convicted.

The auditors found that the CIB provided a variety of services to local law enforcement agencies in the state and local police and other criminal justice agencies were pleased with the CIB services. Many areas in the CIB administration and operations, however, needed to be improved. Many aspects of the CIB's operations were loosely managed and often uncontrolled. Beginning with the lack of an adequately defined role for the CIB, the auditors found weaknesses that extended to such basic issues as the improper use of undercover funds. Much of the work performed by the CIB investigators was inconsistent with the CIB's perceived role. Instead of focusing on major cases, the CIB expended significant manpower and resources on minor ones. Comparing CIB investigations to those of other investigative agencies, the auditors found that the CIB investigations were not as successful. In analyzing the CIB's performance, the auditors found that Maricopa County prosecutors refused to prosecute CIB cases more often than similar cases prepared by four other Maricopa County agencies. A major factor in the CIB's lower prosecution rate was the Bureau's failure to conduct case follow-ups necessary to assist in the prosecution. The auditors also found that CIB officers were allowed to initiate cases as they chose. The CIB management did not adequately track and oversee the cases under its investigations. CIB officers' casework was poorly documented. The department had been placing personnel in CIB management positions who at the time of placement had no experience conducting narcotics or intelligence investigations. Investigators spent undercover funds on inappropriate items other than those intended and flash roll monies were issued without proper approvals.

The auditors suggested that the Criminal Investigation Bureau could potentially fill a unique and important role as the State's only statewide investigation function. They recommended that the CIB define a clear mission for its independent investigative functions and communicate this mission to the law enforcement and prosecuting agencies in the state. The CIB management needs to define clearly what types of service requests from outside agencies it would respond to, and when and how the priority of service requests would affect officers' responsibilities in nonservice request investigations. The CIB should then communicate this position to jurisdictions using their assistance. Once the department has established a clear role for the Bureau, the CIB needs to establish a structure to carry it out and train and technologically equip its officers to do the types of high-level crime investigations viewed as its focus.

To improve its effectiveness, the CIB will need to strengthen the management of almost all of its activities, including case planning and supervision, case file documentation, and preparation of cases for prosecution. To correct deficiencies in its case file documentation, the CIB needs to track cases assigned to officers so that supervisors are aware of those cases that need to be reviewed, require consistent utilization of the file folder checklist, conduct routine supervisory reviews of files to ensure case officers are preparing files in a comprehensive manner, and develop a policy for storage of case files that allows management to retrieve them easily. The CIB should begin to track case outcomes and set measurable goals for improvement. Case disposition should be a required element in the case file and any automated case management system. The CIB management should develop a plan to obtain suggestions and feedback from all prosecuting agencies it works with. In connection with its case tracking system, the Bureau needs to develop a mechanism to capture caseload-by-officer information, which should be used in evaluating officer productivity and effectiveness.

The CIB officers should not be allowed to initiate cases without supervisor approval. The CIB needs to adopt and adhere to the criteria for case planning and initiation. A case initiation form should be used to document the reasons for beginning a case, and the form should be reviewed and approved by the appropriate supervisor when a case is initiated. Case plans should be developed for larger and more complex cases, which should include the reasons for the investigation, resources needed, anticipated results, appropriate management approval, and anticipated costs. Documented supervisory approval should be obtained for continuing work on lengthy cases. The Bureau should take actions to ensure that the automated case management system capture the critical case information necessary for management reports. The system should allow the management to access information such as the number of cases being investigated, the status of those cases, the number of man-hours and resources expended on each case, the number of arrests, and the outcome of each case. Further, the Bureau needs to include all aspects of case planning and initiating as part of the case management system.

The Department of Public Safety (DPS) should consider developing a placement system for CIB management personnel that requires prior experience in investigations of narcotic cases. The CIB needs to strengthen its internal controls over undercover funds and flash roll monies. The DPS should develop controls to ensure that evidence acquisition funds are not misused. Policies and procedures must be followed; expenditure receipts, logs, and fund verifications should be reviewed by a designated independent party; and written authorization should be obtained for the disbursement of flash roll monies. Entities that wish to borrow flash roll funds should agree in writing to reimburse the DPS if any money is lost. A formal time frame should be established for the return of flash roll monies.

The Department of Public Safety responded to the audit findings and recommendations by stating that in many areas the agency had identified the problem or deficiency prior to the audit and had taken or was taking appropriate measures to correct or enhance performance in those areas. In general, the DPS believed that the audit report served to only validate the corrective measures the agency had taken in their effort to improve the function, efficiency, and management of the CIB. It concurred with the needs to define more clearly its role as the State's investigative bureau and had taken steps to institute appropriate organizational and philosophical changes to address the concerns. As a result of the most recent reorganization, substantial manpower and financial resources had been focused on major investigations in balance with a commitment to task forces and some street-level operations. The agency, however, considered that the assertion that DPS cases were filed at a rate lower than that of other units was inaccurate. In the area of case documentation, the agency considered it difficult to respond to the generic comments but indicated that the CIB defined the closure of a case at a point when charges against all defendants were adjudicated. And there existed a joint responsibility for case prosecution, shared equally between the law enforcement officer and the prosecutor.

Audit of Financial Management. The United Kingdom has a centralized police system in which financial responsibilities at the central command do not necessarily align with operational decision-making. Although this problem is directly associated with the centralized nature of a police system, the issue is relevant also to large police agencies in the United States. Overall, local forces or commanders need to have greater responsibilities for financial management and greater scope and incentives for practicing it. To do so, they should have better financial information about where costs are incurred, increase value for money by reducing waste, and improve compliance with centrally determined budgets. In this audit, the Audit Commission (1991) reviewed the financial management practices of local police forces in England to determine their financial management status and cost effectiveness.

The commission found that centralized financial control brought with it a number of problems. It introduced delays and uncertainties, making it difficult for local commanders to adapt to changing needs. Suboptimal decisions were often made because the central police command did not always have good knowledge of the local circumstances. Police services were not fine-tuned to local needs and circumstances because a local police commander had not been delegated with both operational and financial control. There was inadequate information on where and why costs were incurred. And there were no incentives provided to local commanders for increasing efficiency.

The Audit Commission recommended that the local forces practice a financial management program that ensures that those police managers who make operational decisions do so knowing their financial implications and accepting responsibility for them. Since financial responsibility should align with operational responsibility, police forces should give subdivisional commanders the management information necessary for understanding the financial implications of their decisions and help them contribute to the framing of force policies and resource allocations. This can be done in the form of a monthly financial summary.

The Audit Commission pointed out the issue of resistance to practicing the local financial management program due to objections to or concerns about local financial management. Some senior police executives, for example, were concerned about compliance with budget control totals after a local financial management program is implemented. To avoid the problems of poor implementation, the Audit Commission recommended that local financial management be tailored to the particular circumstances of a force because there is no standard structure that can be applied universally and be integrated into the overall resource management systems of the force, with particular attention to the annual processes of setting budgets, priorities, and objectives. The force should follow operational command structures in clarifying financial responsibilities. Since clarification of financial responsibilities requires clarification of operational responsibilities, the force should provide operational commanders the management information they require to act as resource managers and should not give them extra administrative duties beyond those implied by their operational responsibilities.

The Audit Commission believed that there are more benefits to individual police managers and police forces from introducing the local financial management program than disadvantages. To individual police managers, it gives management discretion and freedom, emphasizes managing as opposed to administration, provides incentives, recognizes good management, and rewards innovation. To the force, it increases motivation of managers, allows police headquarters to concentrate on key issues, encourages efficient use of resources, provides information on where money has been spent, and allows comparison of management performance.

The Audit Commission also recommended that the force establish a financial specialty at the force headquarters to instigate change and support budget managers, review the force's financial information system to decide whether it can support the complex operational requirements of the force, introduce a cost center structure that can accurately map the costs associated with territorial and other operational activities, make an agreement on which budgets should be delegated and which should remain centrally controlled since not all budgets should be delegated, allocate one accountable officer for each budget and a clear reporting line of responsibility for budgetary control, reach an agreement on what happens to savings achieved through good financial management, and assess management information needs of all officers responsible for budgets.

Audit of Response to Calls for Service. The public reports a large number of incidents to the local police every year. In London Metropolitan Police, there were about 4.5 million such calls in 1994. This audit of police response to calls to the London Metropolitan Police Service was conducted by the National Audit Office (1995). The National Audit Office examined the speed, efficiency, and effectiveness in answering the calls, the speed and urgency of officers in attending the incidents, and the first actions of officers on arrival. The Metropolitan Police Charter includes performance indicators and associated targets the auditors may use in evaluating the time taken to answer calls and actions taken by officers at the scene of an incident.

The National Audit Office interviewed uniform and civilian staff, examined papers at the New Scotland Yard and six local police stations, accompanied officers on duty and at the scenes of incidents, and observed the operation of the Central Communications Complex and Divisional communications rooms. To provide an external perspective, the auditors examined the approach adopted by the Automobile Association and the London Fire Brigade and compared Metropolitan Police Service targets and performance against those of other major police forces. A consulting agency working with the National Audit Office held a series of controlled focus-group discussions to seek views of those police officers and civilian staff who received reports of incidents. The focus groups explored the ways communications officers and controllers dealt with calls from the public and the factors they took into account in deciding grades of response. The aim of the research was to highlight problems in dealing with public calls, provide the Metropolitan Police with examples of good practice, and help improve the service offered to the public. Five focus groups were conducted in total, with participants recruited in consultation with the Metropolitan Police to fill broad quotas for civilian and police staff, Central Communications Complex and Divisional staff, and new and more experienced staff.

The National Audit Office also commissioned a research company to carry out opinion surveys to gather information on public views of the Metropolitan Police in their response to calls for service. A sample of 1,900 people was selected to gauge performance in answering calls and getting to incidents, assess quality of service provided on arrival, determine whether performance met public expectations, identify causes of satisfaction and dissatisfaction, and gather suggestions for service improvements. Because the police dealt with a wide variety of incidents, to gather views on a consistent basis about the response provided, the National Audit Office decided to focus on the opinions of reporters and victims of burglary, for which the calls were graded as immediate, soon, or extended. The survey research was carried out in two stages. In Stage I, twelve qualitative in-depth interviews were conducted to provide a detailed understanding of issues of concern to reporters and victims and provide information helpful for designing the quantitative questionnaires. In Stage 2, 1,904 telephone interviews were conducted with a randomly selected sample of callers. Each interview took an average of 20 minutes to complete, using Computer Aided Telephone Interviewing. A quota approach to sampling was taken to ensure that an adequate number of immediate, soon, and extended grade calls were included.

The auditors found that the Metropolitan Police answered 80 percent of 999 calls within 15 seconds, 90 percent within 18 seconds for calls to local operator centers, and 60 percent within 30 seconds for calls transferred to Divisional communications rooms. On average during 1994, the Metropolitan Police met its 80 percent target for emergency calls, answering 83 percent within 15 seconds. It also generally met its targets for operator centers and Divisional communications rooms, although not consistently across the year or at all locations. The Metropolitan Police had taken action to address some of the causes of delay by avoiding under- or overstaffing of communications officers on duty and introducing new shift patterns at the Central Communications Complex. The speed of answering calls tended to become slower whenever the Complex was understaffed. At Divisional communications rooms, there were significant differences between workload and staffing. But the scope for improvement was constrained by the fact that all Divisions must have at least two communications officers and a controller on duty at any time regardless of workload. Another situation that gave rise to a number of management problems was that communications rooms were staffed by both police officers and civilians. Police officers were multifunctional and often posted to the communications room for indeterminate periods to fill unexpected absences. Although the Metropolitan Police had a long-standing policy of civilianizing communications rooms, it also believed that there was a need for police officers as controllers in communications rooms to maintain a police presence, take control of emergencies, and ensure that police operations were directed with appropriate authority. In addition, the Metropolitan Police had not yet defined the standard of the caller service that communications room staff should provide when talking to callers.

The Metropolitan Police assessed the urgency of all reported incidents and aimed to assign an appropriate speed of response. For the most urgent incidents, the police aimed to have an officer at the scene within 12 minutes at least 75 percent of the time. For less urgent incidents, where an officer was not sent immediately, they aimed to attend as soon as possible and in any case within an hour. Where a response was likely to be more than an hour, they aimed to make an appointment. Between August 1994 and October 1994, officers attended 91 percent of urgent incidents within 12 minutes. For less urgent incidents, officers attended 90 percent within the intended response time of an hour. The response time was between one and two hours in 7 percent of incidents and over two hours for 3 percent of incidents. There was a wide range of times of arrival for incidents when an appointment was made for an officer to attend. The Metropolitan Police had not yet set targets for keeping appointments or monitored related performances.

There were wide variations in the use of the most urgent grade, "immediate," at the Central Communications Complex. On average 28 percent of incidents were graded "immediate" although significant variations existed between staff. At Divisional communications rooms, there were wide variations in the use of "soon." On average 84 percent of incidents were graded "soon," but the proportion varied from over 95 percent by 15 officers to under 70 percent by 16 officers. Greater consistency was achieved in the use of the "immediate" grade. In addition to the variations between communications officers, there were considerable variations between Divisions, including those with similar numbers and types of incidents.

The National Audit Office provided recommendations for all the areas they had examined. On reporting an incident by telephone, it was recommended that the police do more to publicize the telephone numbers of local police stations so people can use them appropriately. On telephone answering speed, they should train staff at operator centers to minimize possible delays, introduce computerized telephone directories at operator centers, consider introducing a separate target for answering times at local communications rooms, and make wider use of call-logging equipment to identify Divisions not meeting the new target.

On staffing the communications rooms, they should examine how the staffing of shifts at the Central Communications Complex could be reviewed to reflect workload demands more closely. The planned review of the role of communications rooms should include examining the scope for rationalizing the number and size of existing Divisional communications rooms to allow a better match between staffing and workload and generate economies of scale. On managing communications rooms, they should press vigorously ahead with its civilianization program and set a target date for all communications officer posts to be civilianized. The police should introduce regular training for communications officers in how to deal with stress and for controllers in how to manage both civilian and police staff, allow potential recruits to talk to communications officers at the Central Communications Complex to obtain a better understanding of the job, improve the screening of officers on their attitudes toward and aptitudes for communications work, and examine the possibility of transferring administrative work done by communications officers out of the communications room.

On standard of service to the caller, the police should consider training their staff to listen more to the caller and ask questions such as "Is there anything else we need to know?" to improve standards further. They should do more to keep callers informed by telling them how long the police will likely take to arrive and, where an appointment is necessary, providing an explanation to callers and making an appointment for a mutually convenient time. The police should emphasize basic quality concepts to all communications officers and reinforce these concepts through training.

On speed of getting to the incident, it was recommended that the police consider revising the target for urgent incidents by extending it to cover all such incidents. They should formally publish its intended response time, introduce a formal target for the proportion of appointments to be kept, monitor performance against the target, monitor patterns of grading, find out the reasons for unexpected variations, provide better guidance on when the extended grade should be used, and improve training given to communications officers on subsequent changes to the communications system. On handling incidents on arrival, they should extend the good practice of police officers to all calls where this is appropriate and useful. They should examine the options and costs for giving callers follow-up information on how an incident has progressed.

There was a strong consensus of opinions across the five focus groups on many of the issues examined. This consistency suggests that the overall findings of this study were likely to be reliable and carry considerable weight. On graded response, apart from recently trained communications officers, few claimed they were briefed fully on graded response and this resulted in differing interpretations of its objectives and the guidelines for grading. The widespread view was that there were problems with the way graded response was implemented in practice. A two-dimensional grading system where calls were perceived as urgent (immediate) or nonurgent (soon) seemed to be used in practice. On pitfalls to avoid in dealing with the public, participants identified insufficient questioning, poor manner, and lack of empathy as the main problems to avoid. The participants also stressed the importance of maintaining high-quality standards when dealing with callers. On training, many civilian participants expressed the need for more practical "on-the-job" training and ongoing "staged" training with emphasis on law and procedures. Police participants felt the need for more training in using the computer system.

Compliance Audits

Compliance audits cannot be completely separated from efficiency or effectiveness audits. They share the goal to ensure that police accomplish their efficiency and effectiveness but are focused on the requirements of laws and regulations in achieving the goal. Compliance auditors, therefore, are equally concerned with matters of economy and efficiency and program results and effectiveness, but approach these matters from a legal and regulatory perspective. In this section, several compliance audits are introduced that address the issue of violations of rules, regulations, laws, and policies in policing. They include audits of compliance with arrest counting rules, criminal incident recording policy, uniform crime reporting guidelines, and use of force laws.

Audit of Police Arrest Statistics. Crime and arrest statistics can be manipulated to create a more positive appearance of police performance records. Crime and arrest counting rules may also be violated because of the complexity and ambiguity of the rules themselves. A variety of strategies for ensuring compliance with the FBI counting rules have been implemented, including training opportunities for police clerks, regular audits, and continuing review of statistics supplied by police agencies. This audit, conducted by the Police Foundation, addresses the issue of compliance with police arrest recording policy at the national level in 1980 and 1982 (Sherman & Glick, 1984).

The auditors used a variety of methods to assess the quality of arrest data and measure the level of compliance with the FBI counting rules. They visited 18 police departments from the Middle Atlantic, Rocky Mountain, and Pacific regions of the United States. The site visits produced a set of questions for state agencies gathering local police statistics. One official per state was asked to complete the questionnaire at the National Uniform Crime Reporting Conference of State UCR Officials. A mailed survey was also conducted with 213 city, county, and sheriff's departments, completed by the heads of police crime-reporting sections.

The auditors found that state UCR agencies allocated relatively little resources to regulating arrest statistics and they did not routinely conduct comprehensive tally checks for arrests in all offense categories. The regulators themselves often failed to recall the UCR counting rules as a majority of the questions included to test state agency knowledge of UCR procedures were answered incorrectly. This weak regulatory system allowed a fairly high rate of errors in definitions used for counting arrests and a very high tabulation error rate for certain offenses in local police departments. The audit identified three state-level strategies for achieving compliance, i.e., training, report review, and auditing. The respondents claimed they had identified several areas of poor compliance by police record keepers. Some police departments encountered problems in reporting racial classifications for non-Black minority groups, some took credit for arrests made by other agencies, and some were not reporting arson arrests made by fire officials. Only 26 of the state agencies reported the existence of procedures for reviewing arrest statistics, and 19 agencies indicated that they counted adult arrests by using the standard FBI definition of adults as persons 18 years of age or older.

Local police departments generally indicated poor compliance with major rules of arrest counting. None of the field visits revealed any department that counted arrests without a formal booking process in a police facility. This nearly universal practice violated the UCR manual of 1980, which asked departments to count arrests of those persons arrested and released without a formal charge placed against them. A variation exists in arrest-counting procedures between police departments that could be attributed to different policies governing supervisory review of arrests. In addition, there were errors across agencies in reporting multiple charges, summonses and citations, and arrests in other jurisdictions. Furthermore, most departments routinely maintained two or three sets of arrest statistics—one for UCR reporting, one for administrative purposes, and perhaps one for public-relations purposes. The administrative reports were often compiled from officer activity logs, and because of this, departments using two-officer patrol cars counted many arrests twice.

The audit findings indicate that arrest statistics were not comparable across police departments because there was a widespread violation of the rules and procedures established by the FBI for compiling arrest statistics. An intensive examination of arrest record-keeping in four diverse police departments found that two departments reported fewer arrests than they actually made and another department reported 14 percent more arrests than it actually made. The findings suggest that the regulation of arrest statistics was extremely weak and that pressures for deviation from counting rules overwhelmed the available strategies for obtaining compliance with those rules. Although an arrest was almost uniformly defined as "booking and charging," compliance with other counting rules varied so significantly that major questions had to be raised about any use of arrest statistics. The substantial number of internal counting errors revealed by the study suggests that departments typically did not care enough about these data to confirm them. As the auditors found, the difference between the arrest totals reported by departments to the UCR system and the number of arrest reports counted by the auditors over the same time period was striking.

Audit of Detective Division Reporting Practices. A serious issue in crime-reporting practices is that police detectives may make deliberate efforts to lower crime statistics by falsely reporting the results of their investigations. Instead of complying with the crime classification procedures, they may erroneously wipe crimes off the books. This audit, conducted by the Auditing and Internal Control Division of the Chicago Police Department (1983a), examined the crime reporting practices of the Chicago Detective Division. Its purpose was to determine if members of the Detective Division possessed workable knowledge of established policy and uniform crime-reporting guidelines related to unfounded criminal incidents.

The auditors examined the Department's UCR monthly "Return A" data for years 1978 through 1982 in an effort to determine if there were appreciable differences in the statistics for those years. Every case and supplementary report was examined and the victim or complainant relative to the circumstances of the incident was interviewed. A search of the Department records determined the size of the population, which was defined as all rape, robbery, burglary, and theft cases that were classified as unfounded by detectives between January 4, 1982 to November 10, 1982. A sample of 2,368 cases was selected. After the sample cases were drawn, the cases and their corresponding supplementary reports were retrieved from the Records Division files, photocopied, and delivered to the audit team. The Detective Division's period activity report, which was compiled every 28 days, was also examined. The total number of cases classified as unfounded for the eleven periods involved was subsequently determined. To verify this information, the Data Systems Division was asked to generate a similar report by computer.

To ensure consistency among the auditors, an audit questionnaire was developed. Discussions between the auditors narrowed the questions to those essential for capturing desired data. The questionnaire to be completed by an auditor eventually required the following information: Records Division number of the case; the crime code; the name of the person interviewed by the auditor; the date, time, and manner of the interview; whether the victim supplied a phone number on the original case report; whether the victim was contacted by a detective concerning the present case; how that contact, if any, was made; the type of investigation conducted by the detective; and the auditor's findings as to whether the detective's conclusion was supported, not supported, or not determinable.

It was determined that a pretest of the audit methodology and questionnaire might be helpful in identifying any problems unforeseen by the audit team. The pretest involved the use of the computer-generated listing of Records Division numbers. Two cases of each type for each area were selected randomly. Rapes in Area 3 were excluded due to the extremely small number. The result was a pretest sample of 46 cases. The auditors then contacted the complainants or victims using telephone and/or personal interviews. The audit began with the first phone interviews in the Second Police District on January 24, 1983. In each case selected for examination, an attempt was made to interview the victim. In cases where phone contact was not made, a visit was made to the victim's home or employment address. Only when no contact was possible was a case listed as not determinable.

To make the necessary assessment of the level of understanding possessed by members of the Division, a series of personal interviews were conducted. These interviews lasted approximately 15 minutes each and were held at the detectives' unit of assignment. The auditors randomly selected the interviewees from among those detectives present for duty on the date of the interview. After preliminary questions on their assignment, length of service in that assignment, and specific duties, the key question was posed: "What are the guidelines that you use to determine that a crime you are investigating is unfounded?" A total of 36 interviews with detectives were scheduled, 3 from each Property Crimes Unit and 3 from each Violent Crimes Unit of the 6 areas. To clarify the statements of the detectives regarding the value of unfounded reports, interviews were conducted with supervisors to determine the criteria by which individual detectives were evaluated. A total of 12 supervisors were interviewed, including 11 sergeants and 1 lieutenant.

The auditors randomly selected the 6th Police Period of 1982 for examination of multiple clear-up practices. Each piece of paper representing a multiple clear-up was retrieved. These files represented every offense initially reported regardless of when that clearing report was submitted. The auditors retrieved each multiple-cleared file in its totality. The file included the original case report, the closing supplementary report, and the multiple clear-up supplementary report. The total number of cases for the sixth period was 660 and the number of cases cleared on any one report ranged from a low of 4 to a high of 102 cases. The same process of interviews with the complainants/victims as used in the uniformed portion of the audit was followed, except that all interviews were conducted by phone.

In the opinion of the auditors, the facts contained in the supplementary reports did not support the investigative conclusions reached by detectives in 971 cases. The facts did support the investigative conclusions reached by detectives in 431 cases. In 983 cases the auditors were unable to make a determination as to the supportability of the investigative findings due to their inability to contact the victims. The highest percentage of supported cases occurred in the rape category and the lowest percentage of supported cases was in the robbery category. The highest percentage of nonsupported cases occurred in the theft category and the lowest percentage of nonsupported cases was in the rape category. Among multiple clearing reports, the data indicated that in 69.4 percent of the cases examined, the victims were not contacted by the detectives clearing the cases. Since there was no notification, it followed that the victims could not decline to prosecute. In 6.1 percent of the sample examined, the victims were contacted and afforded an opportunity to prosecute the offenders.

The auditors concluded that, first, the quality of investigations as documented in the detective supplementary reports was in need of improvement. The supervisory review of detective's supplementary reports was inadequate. The accuracy and integrity of the detective supplementary reports suffered because of inadequate supervisory review as erroneous information in the investigative reports was found in the sample. Second, Detective Division crime reporting practices did not provide adequate controls to ensure victim/complainant contact. There existed a perception that detectives were expected to unfound, clear, or reclassify a certain percentage of their cases and that suspended or unsolved classifications ranked lower than other classifications. The detectives displayed an insensitivity to the victim's plight, evidenced by the number of cases that were classified as unfounded because of lack of cooperation. Third, the review process within the case management system was inadequate. The case management system adopted by the Detective Division was intended to streamline paper flow and allow detectives to concentrate on more serious and solvable crimes. Completed investigative reports were often not returned to the case management supervisor. The supervisor therefore could not determine if his assignment strategy was leading to desired results. Although the review function was the responsibility of the administrative section of the area level, the auditors found that the review process focused its concern on form rather than content.

With these findings and conclusions, the auditors recommended that the Detective Division develop an operational procedural manual and distribute it to all personnel of the Division. In addition, a training curriculum should be implemented to familiarize the personnel with all procedures and standards contained therein. The manual should address and establish proper reporting and investigation procedures, crime classification policies and criteria, standard report formats, detective evaluation system, line internal controls to ensure integrity of the crime reporting system, and any other information pertinent to Division operations. Performance standards for detectives should also be established and documented and all detectives should be informed of how these standards will affect their evaluation. In establishing these standards, commanding officers should consider their effect on detectives' performance. All levels of command and supervision of the Division should be required to conduct and document tests on the integrity of the evaluation system as part of their regular duties. To improve the case management system, case reports should be selected at random and victims interviewed to verify information contained therein. If erroneous information is discovered, training and/or disciplines should be utilized. The Detective Division should develop a case management system with weighted solvability factors and responsive feedback systems and implement a system of internal control relative to multiple clearing reports. The Auditing and Internal Control Division should also conduct periodic preannounced and unannounced audits of the Detective Division.

The auditors believed that the implementation of these recommendations would result in a noticeable rise in the reported crime rate. This rise, however, would be a one-time occurrence as the rate would reach its valid level. Once that level is reached, it would accurately reflect the true rate of criminal activity in the city. The system would have built-in controls to ensure integrity and accuracy of crime rate data that it generates. Subsequent changes in the crime rate would then be a function of the societal factors that affect it rather than a function of the reporting process. Additionally, this crime rate data should enable police planners to more accurately assess and evaluate police manpower requirements and deployment, crime pattern information, and other research that is dependent upon accurate crime reporting.

Audit of Uniform Crime Reporting. This audit by the Auditing and Internal Control Division of the Chicago Police Department (1983b) was a further inquiry into crime reporting integrity and compliance after the audit of the Detective Division reporting practices. The purpose was to determine the basic procedures utilized for ensuring compliance with uniform crime reporting guidelines by major metropolitan police departments, identify common and disparate techniques, and assess and compare them with the International Association of Chiefs of Police (IACP) standards (see Technical Research Services Divisions, 1976). Police auditors from the Auditing and Internal Control Division of the Chicago Police Department visited and audited 7 major police departments, including New York, Los Angeles, Chicago, Philadelphia, Houston, Detroit, and Milwaukee.

The auditors developed a questionnaire utilizing a series of basic questions regarding the systems, techniques, and methods employed in crime reporting by the police agencies to the FBI. On-site interviews were conducted with department representatives ranging in rank from senior police officials to mid-management supervisors to line personnel. Directives and manuals were reviewed and any unresolved questions that arose were answered. Back in Chicago, the auditors compiled their collective data and developed supporting graphs and charts reflecting the systems they had audited.

They found that what was ultimately reported could be distorted by individuals working within the system due to various decision points and definitions of crimes. In their analysis, they identified at least 12 decision points where reported crimes could be attenuated. These were emergency telephone operators, dispatchers, communication supervisors, preliminary investigating police officers, field supervising sergeants, district review officers, detective review officers, follow-up investigating detectives, detective supervisors, state attorneys, external reviewers, and UCR statisticians. The definitions of crimes frequently vary between individual states and the FBI. Consequently, reports often had to be adjusted to fit UCR definitions. Internal procedures for classifying crimes also varied from agency to agency. The directives and manuals reviewed reflected basic differences in the rules for reporting crimes. Some jurisdictions permitted crimes to be unfounded if state attorneys declined to prosecute, even when all elements of a crime were present. Others indicated that if the crime was committed by a minor under the statutory age for prosecution, except as a delinquent, it would not be tallied as a crime.

The auditors found that the crime reporting systems within the various police departments generally reflected the management philosophies of those organizations. Great latitude was granted to line personnel in certain jurisdictions in classifications of crimes. In other locations, that task was retained as a near final step in the systems. Some departments depended heavily on immediate supervision to ensure integrity of the systems. Other agencies rigorously audited reports using senior officials or high-ranking members out of the normal chain of command. The integrity of supervision was presumed in certain departments. In others, agencies outside the departments conducted routine recurring audits of reports, bookkeeping practices, and record retention procedures.

The various departments all subscribed to numbering police reports. Some numbered all calls for service. Others relied on computer-assisted record keeping to maintain and retrieve information pertinent to specific incidents. The IACP recommended that all calls for service that require the dispatch or assignment of a police officer receive a control number. Only one of the agencies studied met this standard. The majority assigned a control number when preliminary investigation confirmed that the incident was a Part I or II crime. Other petty matters were often the subject of an unnumbered informal report or a code appended to a computer record.

The auditors made several suggestions on how to improve the crime reporting systems. First, departments should examine and test the decision points to determine the integrity of the systems. These procedures could be created and practiced by auditors from an auditing and internal control unit like that of the Chicago Police Department, which has the knowledge and expertise to conduct meaningful examinations. The auditors employed to examine the systems should be from outside of the reporting chain of command and able to perform their function as disinterested and impartial parties. Second, the imposition of a control number for each and every police incident is unnecessary if adequate means are available to retrieve basic data concerning every reported incident. Third, an independent internal auditor who can apply standard audit practices should periodically test and examine the UCR statistician's work product.

Audit of Police Use of Force. Police use of force incidents, although rarely occurring, often raise issues of police compliance with related laws and regulations and police training. Pursuant to request of the chairman of the Subcommittee on Treasury, Postal Service, and General Government of the House Committee on Appropriations, the General Accounting Office (1996) conducted this audit to identify ATF's policies for the use of deadly force, determine the reasons for and the extent to which ATF used dynamic entry, and assess whether ATF complied with its procedures for investigating shooting and alleged excessive use-of-force incidents. GAO also compared how ATF addressed these issues with the way the Federal Bureau of Investigation and the Drug Enforcement Administration addressed them. The audit of ATF's compliance with its investigative procedures was based on GAO's review of ATF investigative file documentation required by these procedures and applied only to these files.

The audit was made between August 1995 and January 1996 in accordance with generally accepted government auditing standards. Auditors reviewed pertinent Treasury, Justice, ATF, DEA, and FBI policies, procedures, and documents on the use of deadly force and certain relevant U.S. Supreme Court and lower court decisions involving the use of deadly force. They interviewed ATF, DEA, and FBI officials concerning their policies on the use of deadly force; visited the Federal Law Enforcement Training Center (FLETC) and ATF's National Academy; observed firearms training, training facilities, and equipment; and spoke with training officials about the training courses provided to new agents. They reviewed ATF teaching guides and student training materials for ATF's Criminal Investigator Training Course, ATF's New Agent Course, and ATF's manual for its new agents. They identified training objectives dealing with use-of-force issues and course training materials provided to Special Response Teams (SRT) on use of force and deadly force. They compared ATF training materials with relevant Treasury and ATF use-of-force and deadly force policies to determine if training materials complied with those policies. They compared use-of-force course descriptions and types of training provided to new ATF agents to DEA and FBI training officials' descriptions of types of training provided to new DEA and FBI agents.

The auditors identified and reviewed files related to the investigation of reported shooting and use of excessive force incidents during fiscal years 1990 through 1995. Of the 92 investigations, they found that 25 involved allegations of physical abuse of persons and/or property. They reviewed ATF's investigative files for all 38 intentional shooting incidents that were reported to and investigated by ATF as well as for the 25 alleged excessive force incidents they selected. ATF, on average, conducted over 12,000 investigations and arrested about 8,000 suspects during fiscal years 1990 through 1995. In the course of these activities, ATF was involved in fewer than 10 reported shooting or alleged excessive force incidents each year. ATF statistics on suspects arrested from firearms investigations during fiscal years 1990 through 1995 showed that 46 percent of the suspects had previous felony convictions, 24 percent had a history of violence, and 18 percent were armed at the time of their arrests.

The auditors based their compliance determination on whether the information in the files indicated that the investigative procedures had been followed. Overall, ATF's shooting incident procedures were comparable to DEA's and FBI's with two distinctions between ATF and these agencies in the delegation of investigative responsibilities and representation on review boards. ATF complied generally with its investigative procedures and all intentional shootings were justified. Most allegations of excessive use of force were unsubstantiated and ATF sanctioned agents who had engaged in misconduct. In October 1995, Treasury and Justice issued uniform policies governing the use of deadly force for each of their bureaus and agencies. GAO determined that the 1988 ATF use of deadly force policy, which was in effect before the issuance of the October 1995 Treasury policy, was consistent with the 1995 Treasury policy. In addition, ATF's 1988 policy was consistent with FBI and DEA policies that were in effect immediately before the issuance of the 1995 uniform policies.

ATF case agents, including those assigned to Special Response Teams (SRT), were trained in the dynamic entry technique. GAO observed new agent and SRT training sessions where ATF agents made dynamic entries into buildings during practical exercises. According to ATF officials, ATF agents primarily used the dynamic entry technique to gain entry to buildings during high-risk search and arrest situations. The equipment used by ATF, DEA, and FBI during dynamic entries was generally comparable. From fiscal year 1993 through 1995, ATF conducted 35,949 investigations and arrested 22,894 suspects. During this same period, SRTs were deployed 523 times and SRT members were involved in 3 intentional shooting incidents. GAO reviewed available documentation for all 157 SRT deployments for fiscal year 1995 and found that the dynamic entry technique was used almost half the time and was the predominant technique used when an entry to a building was required. However, in none of the 1995 SRT dynamic entries did ATF agents fire their weapons at suspects.

GAO's discussions and review of course materials showed that within the first week of training, each agency provided new agent trainees with a classroom lecture and discussion describing the agency's use-of-force and deadly force policies. Thereafter, each agency integrated use-of-force issues into other segments of the training where force could be a relevant issue. Each agency employed training techniques such as practical exercises that involve the use role-playing and firearms judgment that require shoot or not-to-shoot decisions. Furthermore, each agency trained new agents on how to recognize the perceived level of threat they face and how to respond to it with an appropriate level of force. Also, agents at the qualifications with whom GAO spoke confirmed that the policy was reviewed before every tactical operation. DEA and FBI officials said that deadly force policies were also reiterated at their quarterly firearms qualifications. ATF conveyed its deadly force policies to new agents through training and the types of deadly force training provided to new ATF agents were consistent with the types of training provided to new DEA and FBI agents.

SUMMARY

Some typical police audits published in the United States and United Kingdom were reviewed in this chapter to provide the reader with a sense of how police audits are conducted. These audits were presented under five subsections: financial-related audits, economy and efficiency audits, program results and effectiveness audits, efficiency and effectiveness audits, and compliance audits. Financial-related audits share the same standards and procedures with financial statement audits but report on selected programs or units of a police department. The two financial-related audits introduced in this chapter are concerned with the audit of federal law enforcement grants and state-police seized asset revenues. Economy and efficiency audits as applied to the police are often concerned with the police use of human and material resources. Four cases of economy and efficiency audits are briefly described, including audits of police staffing and leave, police manpower, police communications room, and fleet management. Police audits concerning program results and effectiveness are evaluations to determine the extent to which desired results or benefits established by the legislature and/or other authorizing body are being achieved and the effectiveness of organizations, programs, activities, or functions in reaching their objectives and goals. Five police audits concerning program results and effectiveness are covered; these are audits of police training, team policing, police community partnership, child recovery, and fingerprint service. Many performance audits put equal emphasis on reviewing both efficiency and effectiveness of police operations. The three such audits discussed in this chapter are concerned with the criminal investigation bureau, police financial management program, and police answers to calls for service. Lastly, compliance audits ensure that police accomplish their efficiency and effectiveness within the requirement of laws and regulations. Four compliance audits were illustrated, including audits of compliance with arrest counting rules, criminal incident recording policy, uniform crime reporting guidelines, and use of force policies.

REFERENCES

Audit and Internal Control Division. (1983a). Detective division reporting practices. Report by the Bureau of Administrative Services, Chicago Police Department.

Audit and Internal Control Division. (1983b). Uniform crime reporting: Systems analysis, seven major cities. Report by the Bureau of Administrative Services, Chicago Police Department.

Audit Commission for Local Authorities in England and Wales. (1990). Calling all forces: Improving police communications rooms. *Police Papers*, 5. London: HMSO.

Audit Commission for Local Authorities in England and Wales. (1992). Audits of key functional areas. London: HMSO.

Audit Commission for Local Authorities and the National Health Service in England and Wales. (1991). Pounds and coppers: Financial delegation in provincial police forces. *Police Papers*, 10. London: HMSO.

Block, P. B., & Ulberg, C. (1974). Auditing clearance rates. Washington, D.C.: Police Foundation.

Comptroller General of the United States. (1980). Report to the Congress: Improved grant auditing and resolution of findings could save the Law Enforcement Assistance Administration millions. Washington, D.C.: U.S. General Accounting Office.

General Accounting Office (GAO). (1994). *Government auditing standards.* Washington, D.C.: U.S. Government Printing Office.

General Accounting Office (GAO). (1996). Use of force: ATF policy, training and review process are comparable to DEA's and FBI's. Report to the Chairman,

Subcommittee on Treasury, Postal Service, and General Government, Committee on Appropriations, House of Representatives. Washington, D.C.: U.S. General Accounting Office.

Hargie, O., & Tourish, D. (2009). Communication and organizational success. In O. Hargie & D. Tourish (Eds.), *Auditing organizational communication: A handbook of research, theory and practice.* New York, NY: Routledge.

Kim, W., & Mauborgne, R. (2003). Tipping point leadership. *Harvard Business Review,* April, 60–69.

Legislative Commission on Expenditure Review. (1986). Local police training. Albany, NY: The Legislature, State of New York.

Legislative Commission on Expenditure Review. (1991). Memorandum report to the Legislature: State police seized asset revenues. Albany, NY: The Legislature, State of New York.

Legislative Division of Post Audit. (1993). Performance audit report: Reviewing the effectiveness of the capital area security patrol. Topeka, Kansas: State of Kansas.

Lester, C. L. (1993). Performance audit of the statewide law enforcement radio system as administered by the Division of Communications within the Department of Management Services. Tallahassee, FL: State of Florida Office of the Auditor General.

National Audit Office. (1992a). *Civilianization of police posts in the Royal Ulster Constabulary.* Report by the Comptroller and Auditor General. London: HMSO.

National Audit Office. (1992b). *Control of police manpower in Scotland.* Report by the Comptroller and Auditor General. London: HMSO.

National Audit Office. (1992c). *Reducing crime in London: A study of the partnership and other methods used by five Metropolitan police divisions.* Report by the Comptroller and Auditor General. London: HMSO.

National Audit Office. (1995). *Metropolitan police service: Responding to calls from the public.* Report by the Comptroller and Auditor General. London: HMSO.

Norton, D. R. (1992). Performance audit: Department of Public Safety, Criminal Investigations Bureau. Report to the Arizona Legislature by the Auditor General. Phoenix, AZ: State of Arizona Office of the Auditor General.

Regan, E. V. (1991). More New York City transit police officers could be made available to patrol the subways. Report 91-S-53. Albany, NY: State of New York, Office of the State Comptroller, Division of Management Audit.

Sherman, L. W., & Glick, B. D. (1984). *The quality of police arrest statistics.* Washington, D.C.: Police Foundation.

Technical Research Services Division. (1976). *The IACP-UCR audit/evaluation manual.* Gaithersburg, MD: International Association of Chiefs of Police.

Templeman, D. W. (1992). Management audit: State Police I Search program. Report by Performance Audit Division, Office of the Auditor General, State of Illinois.

Chapter 6

INDEPENDENT POLICE AUDITORS

Police audits are traditionally conducted by a city or its parent government's accounting and/or audit division or controller's office, by accounting and/or auditing staff within a police department, or by an auditor outside the government, i.e., a private accounting firm. The auditor of the City of Dallas, Texas, for example, audited the Dallas Police Department's Employee Morale Fund, a cash fund, including its processing duties and monitoring and supervisory controls (Kinton, 2010). The New Jersey State Commission of Investigation reviewed police pension systems, compensations and benefits, and civilianization in New Jersey municipalities (New Jersey Senate Community and Urban Affairs Committee, 2010). An example of an internal audit is the Freeborn County, Minnesota, Domestic Violence Safety and Accountability Audit. This audit reviewed the overall response to domestic violence and was performed by a 9-member audit team comprised of practitioners from within the county's criminal justice system, i.e., 911/dispatch, law enforcement, prosecution, jail, and probation (Freeborn County Audit Team. 2004). Occasionally, a law enforcement officer from another jurisdiction is requested to conduct a police audit. Scott Roy, an officer from Culpeper, Virginia, inquired about Quantico Police Department's management of drugs, cash, and handguns, processing of evidence and cash, and handling of service calls (Borden, 2013). Other cases of police audits by outsiders involve the use of an external accounting and/or consulting firm. One such firm examined the investigative reports of two Pasadena Police detectives, whose conduct was called into question by a superior court judge, including withholding evidence that supported the innocence of a defendant and misconduct in the recorded interview of a witness (Healy, 2013). Another external consulting firm from Rio Rancho, New Mexico, audited Portales Police Department's culture, communication, and handling of evidence (Associated Press, 2012). And StoneTurn Group LLP examined the Vermont State Police payroll and overtime pay and related approval process (Birkshire Eagle Staff, 2013).

The position or Office of the Independent Police Auditor (IPA) is a relatively recent development in the field of police auditing. Different from traditional audit functions performed by a city or state government auditor, an internal police auditor, or an external auditor, an Independent Police Auditor (IPA) occupies a largely self-governing municipal office that specializes in auditing police investigations of citizen complaints. It has been established as an external oversight body that monitors police activities and determines if a police investigation is complete, thorough, objective, and fair, and thus serves as a resource for citizens of a city regarding police actions and standards (City of Tucson, 2013).

The Office of the Independent Police Auditor (IPA) has been created primarily in response to inadequacies, perceived or real, associated with traditional police oversight mechanisms and the need to prevent legal liabilities and save tax dollars. Police internal probe has been questioned because the same officer who ordered the operation might be involved in the internal inquiry. In such situations, a police department often faces criticism for its handling of the incidents, especially when they are controversial (Bhattacharjee, 2010). The public and community activists are the driving force behind the creation of the IPA as they demand protection of citizens' rights and consequences for police misconduct and see that the only way to achieve this is through the investigations of an independent auditor. Another major incentive for creating the IPA position is to prevent legal liabilities as many cities face potentially costly civil lawsuits against their police departments. The IPAs do not come easily, however. It took years of public protests and debates, for instance, for the Fresno City Council to finally approve the hiring of an auditor to look into police shootings (Dorland, 2011).

Office Structure and Auditor Qualifications

The Office of the Independent Police Auditor (IPA) is established through directives of a city council or mayor and reports usually directly to the city council or mayor. The creation and operations of the office is governed by a city charter section or ordinance. An independently appointed audit committee is responsible for the appointment and termination of an IPA, thus providing the independence necessary for objectivity in compliance with the Generally Accepted Government Auditing Standards (GAGAS). A city council or a public safety committee comprising councilmembers may be charged with the responsibility to evaluate the activities of the Independent Police Auditor.

Titles of the Office of the IPA vary from city to city as the Office of Independent Review (Fresno, CA), Office of the Independent Monitor (Denver, CO), Independent Police Review Authority (Chicago), Office of Independent Police Review, Office of Professional Accountability, and Ombudsman have all been used. Several models have emerged that suggest different structures the Office of the IPA may operate under. One model allows the IPA to work as a separate agency in a city government. In Chicago, for example, the Independent Police Review Authority (IPRA) was created and approved by the City Council in response to concerns about investigations of allegations of police misconduct by the Chicago Police Department. Headed by a civilian Chief Administrator and staffed entirely with civilian investigators, the IPRA is an independent agency of the City of Chicago, separate from the Chicago Police Department.

Another model requires that the IPA works under and provides support to a civilian review board. Because the civilian review board functions independently and reports directly to and is funded by a city council, the IPA is also considered independent. In Eugene, Oregon, for example, the police auditor supports the Civilian Review Board (CRB), which provides input about fairness, completeness, and thoroughness of the police investigative process. The Board consists of seven members from the community appointed by the City Council, whose goal is to make the system of police accountability more transparent and increase public confidence in the manner that police conduct their work. Similarly, the Office of the Independent Monitor in Denver, Colorado, operates under the Citizen Oversight Board (COB), which consists of seven residents appointed by the Mayor and confirmed by the City Council (Office of the Independent Monitor, 2012).

A third model blends the review, monitoring, and auditing/ombudsman functions within one city government. The Seattle City

Council created such a hybrid accountability system in 1999, which includes a civilian review board, a civilian director, and a civilian auditor (Bhattacharjee, 2010). The Office of Professional Accountability Review Board consists of seven citizens appointed by the City Council. The Director of the Office of Professional Accountability (OPA) oversees the Seattle Police Department's Internal Investigations Section and reports to the Chief of Police. The Office of Professional Accountability (OPA) auditor is an independent civilian contractor appointed by the Mayor and confirmed by the City Council (Office of Professional Accountability Review Board, 2013). The OPA auditor casts the first civilian eye on an investigation, before the Review Board or the Director, and performs audits of all complaints and investigations (Bhattacharjee, 2010).

Qualifications of the IPA vary from city to city but usually include backgrounds in law, law enforcement, and the judicial system and experience in police auditing and reviews, besides appropriate education and training credentials. Veteran police officers who have served at the local or state level, police instructors from colleges and universities, attorneys with law enforcement background and police auditing experience, veteran FBI agents, and criminal court judges have all served as IPAs. For example, the mayor of Seattle seeks out candidates for the civilian auditor position that have a strong background in dealing with criminal cases and the judicial system (Bhattacharjee, 2010).

Functions and Responsibilities

An Office of the Independent Police Auditor (IPA), depending on where it is located, performs at least one or a combination of the following functions or responsibilities. First, it maintains a program of community outreach to inform and educate the public about the Office of the IPA, the complaint process, and related police policies and procedures. For this purpose, its services are structured to support a cooperative relationship of trust and responsibility and promote a partnership relationship in upholding police accountability. Activities in this regard include listening and responding to broader community concerns, soliciting community inputs, maintaining regular communication with members of the public (Office of Professional Accountability Review Board, 2013), and preparing annual and other reports to the community, city government, and the police department.

Second, the IPA reviews, assesses, and monitors police investigation of critical incidents that might involve police misconduct and cause concerns to members of the public. In this area, the IPA provides independent oversight of police complaint investigations to ensure that the investigations are thorough, objective, and appropriate; and that all complaints against police officers are treated fairly and investigated expeditiously. Any case brought forward containing misconduct issues would be classified as a complaint with related allegations, findings, and individual officers tracked. The office thus enhances police accountability and transparency and instills public confidence in the complaint process (Office of Professional Accountability Review Board, 2013). The Office of the Independent Monitor (OIM) in the City of Denver, Colorado, for example, monitors community complaints regarding allegations of police misconduct and Internal Affairs Bureau (IAB) investigations of complaints against Denver police officers. The OIM does not investigate or review the validity of criminal charges brought against complainants. The Citizen Oversight Board (COB) makes policy-level recommendations relevant to the police, addresses any other issues of concern to the community, and reviews and makes recommendations on closed Internal Affairs cases when the findings are not sustained (Office of the Independent Monitor, 2012). An additional benefit of the review and monitoring function is that the Office of the IPA can prevent a city from costly lawsuits by resolving citizen concerns before they reach the courtroom.

Third, the IPA provides independent investigation of citizen complaints filed with the office or participates in investigations of sworn personnel. To achieve this function, it directly accepts complaints of misconduct against police officers and serves as an alternative dispute resolution process for resolving certain complaints. Activities in this regard often involve responding to the scenes of officer-involved shooting incidents and monitoring the ensuing police investigations. Depending on the nature of cases and circumstances, the Office of the IPA may not do its own investigations, however; it would instead send a complaint to the internal investigation unit of the police and allow the police to conduct a formal investigation. Like the second function described above, an alternative channel for citizens to file complaints and for complaint investigations can prove a cost-effective measure to a city if citizen concerns can be resolved through the Office of the IPA.

Fourth, the IPA conducts independent reviews of police policies and procedures and quality of police complaint and investigation process for fairness. In this regard, the IPA carefully considers aggregate data from citizen complaints, community concerns, and public policies in crafting recommendations to the police and city council (City of San Jose, 2013). It may also engage in researching national trends and best practices on police accountability and performances. Such activities are aimed at enhancing police policies and procedures, strengthening police accountability and performances, and improving police hiring and training practices. A city with the Office of the IPA that provides such reviews and oversight is also in a better position to address liability issues arising out of civil lawsuits and thereby save taxpayers' money.

Types of Cases Handled

The IPA handles typically four types of cases: (1) use of unnecessary force or any force citizens believe to be wrong (Dorland, 2011), including use of deadly force, shooting, suspicious and wrongful deaths, Taser maintenance, and Taser deaths; (2) financial-related cases such as officer benefits, police efficiencies and staffing levels, off-the-book accounts involving prisoners and unclaimed cash, special investigation funds, information services center cash collections, impounds and property room, and fleet purchases; (3) misbehaviours such as discourteous treatment, verbal abuse, coercion, racial profiling, sexual orientation bias, and sexual harassment; and (4) routine police operations such as 311 call center operations, domestic violence response, detective bureau reports, criminal case filings (Healy, 2013), and fleet management (Ellis, 2012).

Solutions and Recommendations

Solutions and recommendations the IPA offers can be grouped broadly under two categories, those impacting a police department in general and those affecting individual officers. Those concerning the police in general include (1) changes in police policies and procedures (Office of the Independent Monitor, 2012), especially those involving police misconduct and public complaints (Office of the City Auditor, 2012); (2) improvements in operations such as enhanced supervision, more relevant training, more use of technology, proper scheduling (Dorland, 2011), more accurate record-keeping, better processing of cash, and greater system enhancement; (3) adoptions of alternatives that can be helpful in solving problems–such as the use of mediation when longer processes do not work (Bhattacharjee, 2010); and (4) productions of information such as complaint statistics, investigation and policy reports, and procedural manuals (Office of the City Auditor, 2012). Those having to do with individual officers involve either no actions when complaints are found invalid and dismissed, or various levels of disciplinary actions when complaints are found valid and sustained (Office of the City Auditor, 2012; Office of the Independent Monitor, 2012).

A central theme apparent in all these solutions and recommendations is the resolution of public complaints. A complaint is usually referred to the Internal Affairs Bureau after it is filed with the auditor (Office of the City Auditor, 2012; Office of the Independent Monitor, 2012). In Denver, Colorado, for example, the IAB will review the complaint, attempt to identify the involved officer(s), locate relevant records of the incident, and may interview the complainant(s) if necessary. Once the intake review is complete, the IAB Commander, after consultation with the Monitor, can handle the complaint in any one of the following five ways: (1) informal discussion and/or counseling with the involved officer(s); (2) mediation between community members and officer(s) with the guidance of professional mediators; (3) referral to other more appropriate agencies or offices; (4) decline of a complaint if the complaint is untimely or false, if Internal Affairs does not have jurisdiction over the complaint, and if the complaint is one that must be decided upon through a court process; and (5) formal IAB Investigation (Office of the Independent Monitor, 2012).

The resolution of a complaint in a city with the Office of the IPA usually hinges on a collaborative working relationship between the IPA and the police. The IPA participates in some or all of the interviews and investigations or monitors these activities by reviewing and commenting on relevant documentation. Once an investigation is complete, it is forwarded to the involved officer's commander for review. In Denver, Colorado, the involved officer's commander makes a finding on the complaint, which is then reviewed by the command staff. There are two general findings: (1) sustained, when the officer is found to have violated Denver Police policies or procedures, and (2) not sustained, when the officer acted within the police guidelines or there is not enough evidence to prove or disprove the allegation or the allegation is false. If an allegation is sustained, appropriate disciplines will be imposed. If an allegation is not sustained, the Office of the Independent Monitor notifies the person who filed the complaint regarding the result of the investigation (Office of the Independent Monitor, 2012).

Another example involves the Office of the Independent Police Review (IPR) in Portland, Oregon, which screens the complaints and makes case-handling decisions after completing preliminary investigations. The IPR may be able to resolve a complaint at intake or needs to refer it to the Internal Affairs Division or a Precinct Commander or a Division Captain for further information. It provides mediation or refers the complaint to another agency when such actions are deemed more appropriate. Similar to cases in Denver, complaints are either found valid or dismissed. The complaints are valid if the involved officers are found to have violated the police policies and they are dismissed if the officers' conduct was found consistent with the police policies (Office of the City Auditor, 2012; Office of the Independent Monitor, 2012).

Political and Professional Issues

The tension between political pressures and a professional orientation often characterizes the work of an IPA. The office faces challenges from various stakeholders on the one hand and strives to maintain professional standards and develop investigative expertise on the other. The conflicting demands from different groups and the political pressure exerted on the auditor can be intense. In Eugene, Oregon, for example, the police auditor was scrutinized by advocates of civilian oversight, some of whom are distrustful of the police, while being questioned by other residents concerned that the office can be used unfairly to criticize police officers doing difficult work (Russo, 2009). In San Jose, California, the police, particularly the rank-and-file officers, resent being investigated by any outsider, including the auditor (Stuchinsky, 1996). The police officers' union filed labor grievances over the auditor, claiming that the city should have negotiated labor provisions before implementing certain elements of oversight. The auditor, meanwhile, answered to the elected City Council, which did not always agree with the auditor's view of the issues in the community and ways to address them. Although some members of the Council acknowledged the delicacy of the auditor's role, others viewed the IPA as an advocate that should push for reforms on behalf of a group or individual (White, 2010). Nevertheless, the police seem less antagonistic toward an auditor than the idea of a citizen review board.

Professional issues of the Office of the IPA are often concerned with the IPAs' authorities, professional neutrality and standards as auditors, and experience and expertise as complaint investigators. An IPA is often restricted by the authorities of the office, with little power to make changes to police policies or initiate internal investigations managed by police without the consent of the police department. He or she is only empowered to evaluate internal investigations and make recommendations to the city council and police based on the findings of police investigations. Most police departments use the traditional model of officers investigating other officers. In many cities, the Office of the IPA is unable to actually investigate police shootings, for example; it can only review police reports about the shootings. In situations like Taser-related deaths, an independent review should be done to ensure that police use of force is proper. But, unless a complaint is filed, the IPA does not have the authority to conduct an independent review of a police department's internal investigation (Sanjeev, 2007).

When an Office of the IPA does conduct its own investigations, the auditor is often criticized for lacking investigatory experience or infringing upon police union rules. An IPA with no domestic violence experience, for example, is not believed capable of investigating domestic violence cases. The police unions often view IPA investigations as interfering with police investigations and cite the union contract as giving police detectives specific investigatory rights. Facing these challenges, some IPAs have demanded more authority and investigative powers, but such attempts have been largely unsuccessful (White, 2010).

Another professional issue of the Office of the IPA is concerned with measurement or evaluation of an IPA's performance. While a city council or a higher city unit such as a public safety committee and the Citizen Oversight Board (COB) is usually charged to direct the functions and operations of the IPA office (Office of the Independent

Monitor, 2012), no standards have been developed for assessing the effectiveness of the IPA. One proposal for measuring an IPA's effectiveness involves examining the results of the audits on police over time, by seeing whether the quality of police investigations has improved, whether the police conduct more thorough investigations, interviewing all the witnesses and collecting all the evidence, for instance. This information is difficult to obtain, however, due to the long time frame required for such an impact to be discernible and the dependency on the police for the evaluative data. Without such information, a city including the city council, the public, and the police simply cannot make a determination as to whether and how the IPA has made a difference. Because the impact of the IPA is difficult to measure and related information hard to come by in a short time frame, a more immediate way for evaluating an IPA's job is to look at his or her activities and achievements, including effort to educate the public, openness of the complaint process for residents (Stuchinsky, 1996), strategies proposed for reforming the police, channels created for improving police-community relationship, and reports prepared and data compiled on complaints that have been made available to the public.

SUMMARY

The Independent Police Auditor (IPA) is a relatively recent development in the field of police auditing. Different from traditional audit functions performed by a city or state government auditor, an internal police auditor, or an external auditor, an Independent Police Auditor occupies a largely self-governing municipal office that specializes in auditing police investigations of citizen complaints. It has been established as an external oversight body that monitors police activities and determines if a police investigation is complete, thorough, objective, and fair, and thus serves as a resource for citizens of a city regarding police actions and standards.

The Office of the Independent Police Auditor (IPA) has been created in response to inadequacies in traditional police oversight mechanisms and the need to prevent legal liabilities arising out of civil lawsuits against local police departments. The IPA position remains in the early stage of its development, is absent in most cities, and had taken years of public protest and debate for cities that do have it to bring it to reality. The Office of the IPA is established through directives of a city council or mayor and reports directly to the city council or mayor. The creation and operations of the office is governed by a city charter section or ordinance. Titles of this office may vary from city to city as the Office of Independent Review, Office of the Independent Monitor, Independent Police Review Authority, Office of Independent Police Review, Office of Professional Accountability, and Ombudsman have all been used.

Several models have emerged that suggest different structures the Office of the IPA may take. One model allows the IPA to work as a separate agency in a city government. Another requires that the IPA works under and provides support to a civilian review board. A third model blends the review, monitoring, and auditing/ombudsman functions within one city government. The qualifications for those holding the IPA positions have not been standardized but usually include backgrounds in law, law enforcement, and the judicial system and experience and/or expertise in police auditing and reviews, besides relevant and appropriate education and training credentials.

The Office of the IPA performs at least one or a combination of the following functions or responsibilities. First, it maintains a program of community outreach to inform and educate the public about the Office of the IPA, the complaint process, and related police policies and procedures. Second, it reviews, assesses, and monitors police investigation of critical incidents that may involve police misconduct and cause concerns to members of the public. Third, it provides independent investigation of citizen complaints filed with the office or participates directly in investigations of sworn personnel. Fourth, it conducts independent reviews of police policies and procedures and quality of police complaint and investigation process for fairness.

The IPA handles typically four types of cases: (1) use of unnecessary force or any force citizens believe to be wrong, including use of deadly force, shooting, and suspicious and wrongful deaths; (2) financial-related cases such as officer benefits, police staffing levels, off-the-book accounts, and impounds and property rooms; (3) misbehaviours such as discourteous treatment, verbal abuse, coercion, racial profiling, and sexual orientation bias; and (4) routine police operations such as call center operations, domestic violence response, and detective bureau reports.

Solutions and recommendations the IPA offers for handling these cases can be grouped broadly under two categories, those impacting a police department in general and those affecting individual officers only. Those concerning the police in general include changes in police policies and procedures, improvements in police operations, adoptions of alternatives that can be helpful in solving problems, and productions of complaint statistics and investigation reports. Those having to do with individual officers involve either no actions when complaints are found invalid and dismissed or various levels of disciplinary actions when complaints are found valid and sustained. The resolution of a complaint usually hinges on a collaborative working relationship between the IPA and the police. The IPA participates in some or all of the interviews and investigations or monitors these activities by reviewing and commenting on relevant documentations.

The tension between political pressures and a professional orientation often characterizes the work of an IPA. The office faces challenges from various stakeholders on the one hand and strives to maintain professional standards and develop investigative expertise on the other. The conflicting demands from different groups such as civil rights activists, city council members, and police union leaders can be intense and the political pressure exerted on the auditor can be daunting. Professional issues involving the Office of the IPA are often concerned with the IPAs' authorities, professional neutrality and standards as auditors, and experience and expertise as complaint investigators. An IPA is often restricted by the authorities of the office, with little power to make changes to police policies or initiate internal investigations managed by police. When the Office of the IPA does conduct its investigations, the auditor is often criticized for lacking investigatory experience or infringing upon police union rules. Another professional issue is concerned with measurement or evaluation of an IPA's performance. No standards have been developed for assessing the effectiveness of the IPA. Proposals for such assessment or evaluation include examining the results of the audits on police overtime and reviewing activities and tasks completed by the IPA in shorter time frames.

REFERENCES

Associated Press. (2012). Portales police audit critical of department. *Portales News-Tribune,* April 29. http://www.krqe.com/dpp/news/crime/portales-police-audit-critical-of-dept

Bhattacharjee, B. (2010). Mayor picks ex-judge as new civilian police auditor. *The Seattle Storm,* June 21. http://slog.thestranger.com/slog/archives/2010/06/21/mayor-picks-ex-judge-as-new-civilian-police-auditor

Birkshire Eagle Staff. (2013). Audit finds fault with Vermont state police payroll. *Birkshire Eagle,* February 27. http://www.berkshireeagle.com/ci_22671159/audit-finds-fault-vermont-state-police-payroll

Borden, J. (2013). Quantico police audit finds missing cash, drugs, guns; Officers resign. *The Washington Post,* January 24. http://www.washingtonpost.com/blogs/crime-scene/post/quantico-police-audit-finds-missing-cash-drugs-guns-officers-resign/2013/01/24/0d40fc58-6659-11e2-9e1b-07db1d2ccd5b_blog.html

City of San Jose. (2013). Office of the Independent Police Auditor. http://www.sanjoseca.gov/ipa/

City of Tucson. (2013). City of Tucson Independent Police Auditor. Tusconaz.gov. http://cms3.tucsonaz.gov/oeop/ipa

Dorland, L. (2011). Omaha police chief addresses demand for police auditor: Renewed call for auditor after arrest video surfaces. *KMTV Omaha News,* September 2. http://www.kmtv.com/news/local/129162658.html

Ellis, N. (2012). Police audit identifies possible $81K savings. *ThisWeek Community News,* January 25. http://www.thisweeknews.com/content/stories/pickerington/news/2012/01/24/police-audit-identifies-possible-81k-savings.html

Freeborn County Audit Team. (2004). Freeborn County, Minnesota domestic violence safety and accountability audit. Freeborn County, Minnesota.

Healy, P. (2013). Pasadena turns to outside auditor to probe investigations by detectives named in misconduct. *NBC Los Angeles News,* February 26. http://www.nbclosangeles.com/news/local/Eight-Years-of-Pasadena-Police-Investigations-to-be-Probed-193471521.html

Kinton, C. (2010). Audit of the Dallas Police Department employee morale fund (Report No. A10-008). Dallas, TX: Office of the City Auditor.

New Jersey Senate Community and Urban Affairs Committee. (2010). Testimony regarding the New Jersey State Commission of investigation report: The beat goes on, Waste and abuse in local government employee compensation and benefits, and the New Jersey Department of Community Affairs, Division of Local Government Services' performance audit of the City of Newark. Trenton, NJ: New Jersey Office of Legislative Services, Public Information Office, Hearing Unit.

Office of Professional Accountability Review Board. (2013). Police accountability in Seattle. OPA review board homepage. http://www.seattle.gov/council/oparb/

Office of the City Auditor. (2012). Independent police review executive summary of the annual report 2011. Portland, OR: Office of the City Auditor.

Office of the Independent Monitor. (2012). OIM complaint and commendation form. Denver, CO: City of Denver. http://www.denvergov.org/oim.

Russo, E. (2009). Police auditor learned the job in a divided city. *The Register-Guard* (Eugene, Oregon), June 10. http://www.thefreelibrary.com/Police auditor learned the job in a divided city.-a0203931482

Sanjeev, B. (2007). San Jose police auditor's reform proposals deserve approval. *San Jose Mercury News,* June 21. https://www.aclunc.org/news/opinions/san_jose _police_auditor's_reform_proposals_deserve_approval.shtml

Stuchinsky, L. (1996). Independent police auditor tries to build trust with only the power of persuasion. *Metro: Silicon Valley's Weekly Newspaper,* January 25-31. http: //www.metroactive.com/papers/metro/01.25.96/police-9604.html

White, B. (2010). San Jose police auditor enters the fray: Tense relations between police department and some minority groups make mediator's post a challenge for former judge. *The Wall Street Journal Online,* May 20. http://online.wsj.com /article/SB10001424052748703315404575250341020132152.html

Chapter 7

EVALUATION APPROACHES

U pon completion of a police audit and presentation of an audit report to a police agency and other concerned parties, auditors and/or audit sponsors should expect the police to start implementing the audit recommendations. If the police can make good on the recommendations and bring about meaningful changes, the audited programs or functions should become more economical, efficient, and effective. Police officials and auditors, however, do not always know whether audit recommendations have been implemented and whether a police organization and its programs have improved because formal post-audit evaluations are rarely conducted. This situation can be attributed to many factors. Oftentimes an audit evaluation is simply not on an auditor's agenda; a police audit is considered complete once an audit report is written and submitted to interested parties. Sometimes an audit sponsor does not consider it necessary to do an audit evaluation, assuming that the police will practice all audit recommendations once they receive them. Other times, lacking in resources prohibits an audit evaluation because reviews of the audit process and outcome can be both time-consuming and labor-intensive. At a time when service demand is rising and personnel growth is restricted, the police or the city that sponsors an audit may find it difficult to invest their scarce resources and skilled manpower in audit reviews (Audit Commission, 1991).

A salient issue inherent in all of these problems is a lack of appreciation for follow-up efforts in the form of audit evaluations. It is important to note that an audit evaluation ultimately determines whether an audit has resulted in any meaningful changes in police services. Ensuring simply that an audit itself be a success is not enough. An

149

audit function cannot be a substitute for internal controls. The improvement of police services and prevention of future irregularities lie with police management and their internal controls. Management is not only responsible for the establishment of internal controls but also for "the detection of lapses in control, investigating their causes (such as their inherent ineffectiveness or the failure of subordinates to apply them) and instituting improvements designed to ensure their non-recurrence" (Woolf & Hindson, 2011:13). Without a commitment to following through with the audit recommendations, endeavors and resources that have been put into an audit might have all gone in vain.

Audit evaluation is an action type of social research that evaluates audited police organizations, programs, operations, policies, or functions to determine whether the police have followed or deviated from the recommendations, whether the recommendations have brought about genuine improvement in police services, to what extent the police have changed their old practices, and whether the recommendations are appropriate for the audited agency. Meanwhile, audit evaluators also measure the effects of an audit recommendation in terms of its specific purposes, anticipated outcomes, and/or program criteria by examining how well related elements have worked (Tontodonato & Hagan, 1998). There are two general approaches applicable to evaluating a police audit: process evaluation and outcome evaluation.

Process evaluation attempts to establish causal relationships between audit results and audit inputs and audit implementation activities. Outcome evaluation attempts to establish causal relationships between audit outcomes and audit results. Worded in a different manner, audit inputs and activities should be related to audit results as determined in a process evaluation, and audit results must be linked to audit outcomes as determined in an outcome evaluation (Tontodonado & Hagan, 1998). Evaluators must first understand the audit recommendations, then link them to intended results and outcomes, and specify them in qualitatively and quantitatively measurable terms. These results and outcomes become yardsticks for measuring police performance in implementing audit recommendations. As required in any research endeavor, operational definitions and objective analyses should be used to describe consistently and specifically the results and outcomes and thereby enhance the overall quality of an audit evaluation (Carter & Sapp, 1998). Operational definitions can be described as operational service standards and objectives and should be specified in the evaluation. Where it is necessary to make assumptions or professional judgments about these standards and objectives, this should be stated explicitly. Where the evaluation indicates the need for a change, the benefits expected from that change should be made explicit (Audit Commission, 1991).

One way to differentiate audit results and outcomes is by looking at their time frames in the implementation process. The audit results measure immediate and intermediate objectives to be achieved by the police in a shorter time frame, usually within a year. The audit outcomes measure the more general goals and impact to be attained by the police in a longer time frame, usually after all related recommendations have been implemented. Since audit results and outcomes are related to process and outcome evaluations, the different time frames can be used to differentiate these two types of evaluations. Those that focus on short and intermediate objectives, using police input and activities as measures, should be considered process evaluations, and those that examine longer-term goals and impacts attained after all related recommendations have been implemented should be regarded as outcome or impact evaluations.

A complete evaluation should be programmed at regular intervals to cover both the process and outcome because the outcome cannot be appreciated without knowledge of the process. The process evaluation provides detailed information about police activities as they implement audit recommendations and addresses the processes by which outcomes will be achieved eventually. It provides answers to any questions about police interventions, sometimes called "the programmatic black box," in implementing audit recommendations. By enabling evaluators to identify strengths and weaknesses of the audit program, it is invaluable for determining what have and have not worked (Cordner & Kenny, 1998; Levin 1987; Elliott & Syfert, 1988). The process evaluation, therefore, is necessary for an appropriate interpretation of any outcome evaluation data and increases the usefulness of an outcome evaluation (King, Morris, & Fitz- Gibbon, 1987).

Process Evaluation

Although process and outcome evaluations are closely related in terms of their data, measurement, and analysis, they can be conducted and discussed separately. As a matter of fact, process evaluation is often regarded as the most common type of evaluation research (Tont-odonado & Hagan, 1998). When applied to police auditing, process eval-uation addresses an important aspect of any evaluation, i.e., documenta-tion and analysis of police program development and implementation. It is directed at providing qualitative and quantitative measures of the audit program, its operation, and its immediate outputs. Assessments are made regarding whether police organizational structure, programs, and activi-ties are changed in a manner audit recommendations require and whether expected audit outputs are actually produced.

Process evaluation answers the questions on whether the audit pro-gram was implemented as intended, what specific audit recommenda-tions were implemented, and to what degree they were successfully implemented. The question of construct validity is brought to bear when the evaluator asks questions regarding the audit intentions. This issue can be addressed satisfactorily through measurement of police procedures and intermediate audit objectives because process evalua-tion assesses procedures used by police to attain audit objectives and captures the early development and actual implementation of the aud-it program. It can be used to determine whether police procedures or activities substantively contribute to the objectives, whether they help the police effectively utilize their resources, whether they are coordi-nated with other elements in the audit program, and whether police officers and staff members are properly trained to execute the proce-dures (Carter & Sapp, 1998).

Process evaluation is designed not only to improve construct valid-ity in implementing audit recommendations, but also to help discover why certain audit recommendations worked and others failed. This as-pect of the evaluation involves monitoring audit implementation, which provides feedback that enables police managers to get things back on track when any police activity deviates from the original audit intent. Most evaluations of police programs have been summative and goal-oriented, with the purpose of determining whether a program or poli-cy has achieved its ultimate goals. While such evaluations are desir-able, they do not provide enough information about police interven-tion in implementing the audit program. The police and the evaluator are left with little sense of what went right or wrong. And when audit programs are shown to have failed in achieving their goals, the police do not know whether the failure is due to an inappropriate audit recommendation or police deviation from the recommendation. The former failure would require discarding the recommendation; the latter would require police management actions to improve audit implementation (Fitzpatrick, 1992). Diligent monitoring of audit implementation process would allow the police to pinpoint the causes of the failure and take appropriate corrective actions. Chabotar (1982) illustrated an instance where police officials can diagnose early management problems by an analysis of budgeted versus actual costs. If significant variations are identified in the control process, police management can determine whether the variations are caused by the audit recommendation itself or failure to implement the recommendation properly. They can then seek to improve police performance or reduce cost by reorganizing their organizational structure, altering their priorities, instituting stricter purchasing and reporting procedures, or taking any other corrective actions.

The process evaluation of police audit can begin as early as when audit activities are underway or as soon as the police receive the audit report and start contemplating implementing the recommendations. It should continue until the police complete implementing all audit recommendations that address short-term and intermediate audit objectives. A thorough process evaluation of a police audit, similar to an evaluation of a police program described by Cordner and Kenney (1998), should address the following four areas. First, the environment within which an audit program is designed and implemented should be clearly described to allow interested parties to understand possible environmental factors that may have an effect on implementation of the audit recommendations. Second, the evaluator should explain the process by which the audit is designed and implemented to enable any third party not directly involved in the audit to fully understand how the auditor made the recommendations and how the police reacted to them. Third, the evaluator must continuously measure police operational activities in implementing the recommendations over time to determine if the police have complied with the recommendations and to document any changes that have occurred during the implementation process. Fourth, intervening events, both internal and external to the audit program, should be identified and described that may affect audit implementation and program outcomes.

Specific information or variables related to the audit implementation process that an evaluator collects should be based on the type of audits being evaluated. They may include demographic conditions of the city at the time of the audit, participants in audit development, level of police involvement in audit development, procedures used in developing audit recommendations, manners in which audit findings are presented to the police, ways police responded to the audit findings, programs developed by the police for implementing the audit recommendations, organizational and structural designs, financial and material resource management, police operations such as patrol deployment and problem-solving activities, and a variety of other administrative and managerial activities that have been implemented according to audit recommendations. In addition, cost information should be attached to these variables to help police management ensure that resources are used for the purposes desired and in the amounts originally planned. Cost information also helps uncover any discrepancies between the audit plan and practice. Further, police departments can use cost information to evaluate whether police management has demonstrated "cost consciousness" and the "ability to control operating costs" as part of the criteria in managerial performance appraisals (Chabotar, 1982:10).

Methods that can be used for collecting process evaluation data may be either qualitative or quantitative and oftentimes both. Due to limited resources for process evaluation, an evaluator is often able to use only one of these methods. In choosing these methods, the evaluator must beware of the weaknesses inherent in both qualitative and quantitative measurement. For example, qualitative data collection methods in forms of participant observation, personal interviews, and documentary analysis may not allow an evaluator to observe more police activities, talk to more people, and review more documents than one should. Quantitative methods such as randomized surveys, statistical analyses of police records based on probability samples, and controlled experiments may not provide the evaluator with enough information about how and why things happened. It is therefore desirable to use both qualitative and quantitative methods to reach a better understanding of the audit implementation process.

Among the various techniques that can be considered for collecting process evaluation data, each has its unique strengths that may help facilitate the evaluation activities. Participant observation is appropriate for describing the related activities (Guba, 1987), allowing the evaluator to appreciate the true flavor of the audit and discover the distinctive set of elements that makes the audit work. The technique helps the evaluator understand the phenomenon from the standpoint of the participants and gain critical insight through an examination of the entire context (Weber, 1949; King et al., 1987; Hagan, 1993). Participant observation is not always feasible, however. It can occur only when evaluators are able to participate in police auditing and audit implementation activities or when they have access to the functional activities of an audited agency. An evaluator who serves as a member of an audit team, a city public safety committee, or a municipal budget review committee, for example, is in a perfect position to discuss audit recommendations, monitor their implementation, and in the meantime collect participant observation data. Another situation that makes participant observation possible is when an internal police management committee is established in the audited agency to facilitate the audit implementation process. When such a committee is created, those police officials on the committee will be in an ideal position to conduct participant observation of audit-related implementation activities. The only drawback here is their potential lack of impartiality or objectivity, especially when they are being compared to independent outside evaluators. Nevertheless, both internal and external participants have the opportunity to personally observe how auditors develop their recommendations and how the police react to and implement them. Spending a great deal of time and effort on site observing police operations, they are able to collect the data firsthand.

Similar to participant observation, personal interview and documentary analysis enable an evaluator to keep track of a police department's response to audit recommendations and its developmental changes associated with implementing the recommendations. Interviews may involve asking police personnel and key program participants to describe what implementation activities look like. Because of credibility issues and the need for detailed descriptions of audit implementation activities, interviews should be used mainly to verify or check the consistency of police activity descriptions arrived at through more direct observations and through documentary reviews whenever possible. Documentary sources of information an audit evaluator uses may include official police, city, and census data. Since documents and records regarding an audit program are routinely kept by police, an evaluator should be able to extract from them a substantial part of the data needed to determine what activities have or have not occurred. Documentary research may supplement information obtained from personal interviews and increase credibility of interview information because records are accumulated as evidence of audit events as they occur rather than being reconstructed later (King et al., 1987).

Outcome Evaluation

Outcome evaluation for a police audit establishes causal relationships between audit outcomes and audit results. Since audit results are determined by measurement of police inputs and activities, outcome evaluation should take into account information from the process evaluation about these inputs and activities whenever possible. The process information provides outcome evaluators with knowledge on whether police activities conform to auditors' and management's expectations and whether these activities have influenced the outcomes. The focus of outcome evaluation is determining the effect or impact police audit programs have on targeted variables such as cost reduction and police productivity. The targeted outcome variables are directly related to the objectives and goals the police have set for themselves before starting implementing audit recommendations. To clearly gauge the outcomes of audit programs, evaluators ask two general questions: Has a police department accomplished the audit program goals? What effects does the accomplishment have? When clear-cut answers to these questions cannot be obtained, evaluators examine the degree to which the police department has achieved its goals, the ways programs and resources have contributed to improving the audited areas, and the extent success or failure can be attributed to factors other than the audit program. In the course of this evaluation, evaluators may find either success or failure stories or both. Greater police efficiency and effectiveness would suggest that police should continue their programs and operations guided by the audit recommendations. Low efficiency and poor performance may indicate that they need to develop new initiatives or programs, which could be seeds for further evaluations.

Since outcome evaluation of a police audit is designed to measure the audit program's effects and the extent of goal attainment following the implementation of audit recommendations, the evaluators must define the goal in some qualitatively or quantitatively measurable terms, identify the proper criteria or variables to be used for measuring success in achieving the goal, determine and explain the degree of success, and recommend further actions to attain the goal (Carter & Sapp, 1998). Definition or predetermination of an audit goal can be regarded as an effort to specify the expected or hypothesized effects of an audit program in an objective and measurable statement. The evaluators identify the expected effects by considering the possible benefits of the audit program, the time frames over which they should accrue, and the costs of achieving them. After the effects or benefits and the time frames for achieving them are determined, the evaluators should specify the measurable criteria by which successful audit implementation will be evaluated (Audit Commission, 1991).

It is important for an evaluator to think about these criteria through and specify them in light of desired effects before an evaluation begins. Without predetermined measurable criteria, an audit program simply cannot be evaluated. The evaluator would be left with no standards to follow in making his or her judgment about whether the audit has or has not worked. If this situation is forced upon some evaluators, they may resort to using any measurement criteria they see fit in the context of their evaluation activities. The criteria chosen during rather than before an evaluation may be influenced by political and personal considerations and are prone to producing highly arbitrary evaluation findings.

Outcome evaluation activities usually begin after the police have completed implementing all adopted recommendations. Outcome evaluators then determine if the police have improved their services by monitoring their practices for six to twelve months or longer if resources allow after the audit program is completed. The outcome evaluation can be built on the process evaluation to take advantage of the information already gathered. With the process data, outcome evaluators are more confident in making judgment about the audit outcomes. The two standard elements for an outcome evaluation are collection and analysis of outcome data. These data must be related to the goals and objectives of an audit program in consistency with the expected effects and measurement criteria discussed earlier.

Outcome variables in police audit evaluations include those concerned with management overheads, command responsibilities, matching of resources with demands, and impact on crime and public safety. More specifically, they involve cost comparisons, patrol manpower management, workload distribution, officer use of overtime and sick days, arrest statistics and/or clearance rate, radio assignment, and crime rates. Because costs are often a specific area of concern in police auditing, outcome evaluators should attach information of program costs to accomplishment of program goals whenever possible. If they find that the police have met expected performance levels but at a higher cost to the agency than what was estimated, they may have to find a way to resolve such an issue. It is, therefore, inadequate to assess outcomes without measuring the costs or to calculate the costs without examining the performance (Chabotar, 1982). Either of them will result in an incomplete analysis of police performance and lead to inconclusive answers to efficiency and effectiveness questions that outcome evaluation is required to address. Planning for cost analysis may involve defining purpose and intended users of cost information, determining service and production units for service to be costed, defining personnel and nonpersonnel components of service being costed, appraising existing accounting system, and deciding on extensiveness of cost analysis (Audit Commission, 1991).

The methods used for collecting outcome evaluation data can be either quantitative or qualitative or both. Quantitative methods such as randomized sampled surveys based on standard questionnaires provide evaluators with more objective data. Qualitative methods such as personal observations, interviews, and documentary analyses produce more in-depth information about why and how certain outcomes have occurred. The designs for collecting outcome data, however, should be more quantitative than qualitative if outcome variables are to be objectively and consistently measured. The quantitative designs may include a pre-post design, a time-series evaluation, or an experimental or quasi-experimental design. The pre-post design is the least costly, which involves comparing pre-audit status of a variable being examined with post-audit status of the same variable to see if that variable has been changed. The time-series evaluation extends the pre-post design to at least two time periods both before and after the audit recommendations are implemented to see if the change is accidental or sustainable overtime. An experimental or quasi-experimental design compares the effect of an audited police program with that of an unaudited program or a program that continues its usual practices.

Outcome evaluators, like any social science researchers, must ensure that their evaluations are based on sound methodology, objective data collection and analysis, and clear understanding of the implementation process. As a group of evaluation experts have identified (National Criminal Justice Reference Service, 1979), insufficient literature review, poor research design, poor-quality data, unethical evaluation behaviors, naive evaluation staff, and a focus on methods rather than the process could all contribute to poor evaluations. Evaluators should endeavor to avoid these limitations during audit evaluation and increase the usefulness of their evaluative results by ensuring the quality of the raw data/information collected, appropriateness of the methodology selected, the quality of all portions of the data collection process, and the quality of the analysis and data interpretation (Carter & Sapp, 1998).

Not only are poor outcome evaluations methodologically flawed and incapable of demonstrating what has really happened, they also often result in misleading findings and cause police administration to stray from the right path. They may, for example, indicate that the effects of an audit program are positive when they are actually negative, that an audit program is successful when it actually has failed, or that an audit program is not working when it is actually working to a certain extent. A biased evaluator equipped with poor methodology may suggest that an audit program failed because the audit recommendations are inappropriate, when in actuality it is because the police intervention in implementing the audit recommendations does not have integrity. Evaluations of correctional programs (Martinson, 1974) have suggested that poor intervention in police auditing can occur because the police programs are not administered skillfully and the police officers who are subjected to evaluations have not received enough training and personal support from the police management.

Several techniques are available for increasing the validity of outcome evaluations. First, outcome evaluators should use multiple methods to measure their outcomes whenever possible. These methods include interviews, observations, documentary research, and questionnaire surveys, for example. If information collected from different methods indicates the same results, the validity of audit evaluation findings is increased. Second, evaluators should devote more time to studying audit program process and intermediate outcomes to identify reasons for failure and improve ability to build models of effective programs (Fitzpatrick, 1992). If at all possible, they should conduct both process and outcome evaluations in order to open the black box between pre- and post-audit and explain why and how they have reached their findings. Third, they should examine not only the face but also the content of information collected and check and recheck the same information with different sources. By following these methods, audit evaluators can expect to improve both the validity of their evaluation conclusions and the utility of their evaluations to police managers and policymakers.

SUMMARY

It is difficult, if not impossible, for a police department to know whether its use of audit recommendations has been successful without a systematic evaluation. Audit evaluations are conducted to help policymakers determine if audit recommendations are faithfully implemented and what effects they have produced as a result of their implementation. There are two types of evaluations applicable to policing, process and outcome evaluations. A process evaluation produces data that can be used in making the decision on whether police have genuinely implemented the audit recommendations within specified time frames. The purpose of process evaluation is to assess whether police input and activities related to audit implementation have produced the immediate and/or intermediate results. An outcome evaluation provides information on whether an audit program has brought about improvement in the organization, programs, activities, or functions that have been audited. The purpose of the outcome evaluation is to measure whether police inputs, activities, and accomplishment of immediate and intermediate objectives have produced the desired effects or impacts. Both types of evaluations require careful analysis, a clear appreciation of both qualitative and quantitative measures, and a sound methodology for their effective implementation. Both should be conducted in order to have a complete understanding of audit effects.

Process evaluation of police audit documents and analyzes audit program development and implementation. It provides qualitative and quantitative measures of the audit program, its operation, and its immediate and intermediate outputs. Two key issues for the process evaluation are whether audit recommendations are implemented as intended and whether they have worked. To address these issues, process evaluators investigate the "black box" called police intervention to understand what has really happened in the implementation process. Assessments are made regarding whether police organizational structure, programs, and activities have been changed in the manner specified in the audit recommendations and whether expected audit results have been produced. A process evaluation generally should describe the environment within which the audit program is created and the process by which it is implemented, measure continuously police operational activities in implementing audit recommendations, and identify intervening events both internal and external to the audit program that may have affected the implementation process.

Outcome evaluation of a police audit is designed to measure the audit program's effects and the extent of goal attainment following the implementation of audit recommendations. The outcome evaluators focus on the desired effects or impact police audit programs have on targeted variables, which are directly related to the objectives and goals the police have set for themselves before implementing the audit recommendations. The two major questions outcome evaluators ask are, whether a police agency has accomplished the audit program goals and what effects the police accomplishment has on targeted variables. Major activities outcome evaluators engage in include definition of audit goals, identification of proper measurement criteria for evaluating police accomplishment, specification of hypothesized effects, assessment of police activities that may have led to outcomes, and systematic collection and analysis of outcome data.

There are no clear-cut methods or designs that specifically fit process or outcome evaluation. Both can utilize qualitative and quantitative information for analysis. Nevertheless, qualitative data may be more prevalent in process evaluation due to the need to describe in detail what has happened in the process of implementing audit recommendations. Quantitative data may be more heavily used for outcome evaluation in order to provide objective pre-post data comparisons. Commonly used qualitative data collection methods include participant observations, personal interviews, and documentary and records analyses; frequently used quantitative methods are statistical analyses of sampled records or cases based on randomized selection procedures, questionnaire surveys, pre- and post-audit comparisons, time-series analyses, and experimental or quasi-experimental designs. Process evaluation requires the evaluators to be on site to describe faithfully what has happened during the implementation of audit recommendations. The outcome evaluation, however, requires the evaluators to follow a research design that will pinpoint before/after audit differences. Successful audit evaluations should be based on sound methodology, high-quality data, objective analysis, ethical evaluative behaviors, attention to both process and outcome, use of multiple measures, and validity and reliability of measurements.

REFERENCES

Audit Commission for Local Authorities and the National Health Service in England and Wales. (1991). Reviewing the organization of provincial police forces. *Police Papers,* 9. London: HMSO.

Carter, D. L., & Sapp, A. D. (1998). Community policing evaluation. In L. T. Hoover (Ed.), *Police program evaluation.* Washington, D.C.: PERF.

Chabotar, K. J. (1982). *Measuring the costs of police services.* Washington, D.C.: National Institute of Justice.

Cordner, G. W., & Kenney, D. J. (1998). Tactical patrol evaluation. In L. T. Hoover (Ed.), *Police program evaluation.* Washington, D.C.: PERF.

Elliott, N. C., & Syfert, P. A. (1988). Local government evaluation in an executive environment. In C. G. Wye & H. P. Hatry (Eds.), *Timely, low-cost evaluation in the public sector.* San Francisco: Jossey-Bass.

Fitzpatrick, J. L. (1992). Problem in the evaluation of treatment programs for drunk drivers: Goals and outcomes. *Journals of Drug Issues, 22*(1), 155–167.

Guba, E. G. (1987). Naturalistic evaluation. In D. S. Cordray, H. S. Bloom, & R. J. Light (Eds.), *Evaluation practice in review.* San Francisco: Jossey-Bass.

Hagan, F. E. (1993). *Research methods in criminal justice and criminology.* Englewood Cliffs, NJ: Prentice-Hall.

King, J. A., Morris, L. L., & Fitz-Gibbon, C. T. (1987). *How to access program implementation.* Newbury Park, CA: Sage.

Levin, H. M. (1987). Cost-benefit and cost-effectiveness analysis. In D. S. Cordray, H. S. Bloom, & R. J. Light (Eds.), *Evaluation practice in review.* San Francisco: Jossey-Bass.

Martinson, R. (1974). What works? Questions and answers about prison reform. *The Public Interest,* Spring, 343–369.

National Criminal Justice Reference Service. (1979). *How well does it work? Review of criminal justice evaluation, 1978.* Washington, D.C.: National Institute of Law Enforcement and Criminal Justice.

Tontodonato, P., & Hagan, F. E. (1998). *The language of research in criminal justice: A reader.* Needham Heights, MA: Allyn & Bacon.

Weber, M. (1949). *The theory of social and economic organization.* New York: Free Press.

Woolf, E., & Hindson, M. (2011). *Audit and accountancy pitfalls: A casebook for practicing accountants, lawyers and insurers.* Chichester, West Sussex, UK: John Wiley & Sons.

Chapter 8

CAMDEN POLICE AUDIT

With the discussion of two audit evaluation approaches, process and outcome evaluations, an illustration of how they are applied to a particular police audit is in order. This chapter describes the audit of the Camden Police Department, New Jersey, conducted in late 1995 and early 1996, and its follow-up evaluations. As a comprehensive performance audit, the Camden Police Audit covers a wide range of issues such as organizational structure, management and operations, personnel and hiring, and costs and savings. By examining the process of the police's implementation of the audit recommendations and the outcomes they achieved, this chapter is intended to provide a sense of what a police audit and its evaluations look like. It should be made clear at the outset that the evaluations of the Camden police audit are described in an abbreviated fashion in this chapter for this purpose only.

The information about the Camden Police Audit as presented here is primarily based on data provided by the Camden Police Department and/or collected by the author during 1996 and 1997 after the Camden police received the Camden Audit Report in early 1996. Readers should not make any general inferences from the information presented herein about the current organization and operations of the Camden Police because materials used here are related strictly and applicable only to audit-related police activities during the two years after the Camden police received the audit report. During the two years in 1996 and 1997 and thereafter, many other organizational, administrative, and operational changes, either related or not related to the police audit, have taken place in the Camden police, which are clearly beyond the scope of coverage and discussion in this chapter.

Audit Background

The Camden Police Department had been audited several times over the past four decades. The Public Administration Service, a consulting firm from Chicago, conducted an audit of the Camden Police in 1962 and provided recommendations for radio communications, record-keeping functions, and patrol area alignments. The Delaware Valley Crime Commission and the New Jersey State Attorney General's Office conducted audits in Camden in 1982 and 1986 outlining the duties of the police chief for day-to-day operations. The 1995-96 audit, which this chapter is concerned with, is a comprehensive audit of the entire police department, including its organizational and command structure, its patrol deployment and operations, its effectiveness in dealing with major crimes and violations, and a variety of administrative and managerial issues. These audits of the Camden Police Department over the years trace the development in the field of police auditing from its traditional focus on certain aspects of police management to its current emphasis on overall police efficiency and effectiveness.

The 1995–96 audit of the Camden Police was conducted in response to serious economic, social, and crime problems in the city. Camden encompasses an area of 8.68 square miles and has an estimated population of 87,492, of whom 35.5 percent are under the age of 18. As the poorest city in New Jersey and fifth poorest city in the United States (Shralow, 1996), it has one-third of its residents (30,588) living below the poverty line and 28,418 residing in households receiving public assistance (U.S. Department of the Census, 1990). The bulk of Camden's workforce does not have the professional and technical skills sought by business employers. The city has lost one-third of its population and three-quarters of its manufacturing jobs since 1960. As a result, it has had a steady erosion of its economic and tax base and a high unemployment rate (Rouse, 1996). The city now requires more social services for those residents that are least able to afford them. Politically, Camden had only 27 percent general election turnout among registered voters, which has resulted in the loss of its political clout with those making major decisions in the county that affect the city's life (Rouse, 1996). Consequently, Camden faces budget gaps and struggles each year for adequate funds. The lack of resources has led to operational problems in almost all municipal departments, functions, and programs in the city (Riordan, 1996).

In the area of public safety, the number of index crimes (i.e., murder, rape, robbery, aggravated assault, burglary, theft, and auto theft) per 1,000 population and the number of index crimes per police officer during the year before the Camden police audit were the highest of all major urban cities in New Jersey (Division of State Police, 1994). Besides index offenses, there were 3,605 domestic violence incidents reported, which equate to 10.3 per police officer, almost three times the major urban average of 3.8. In 1994, the year before the audit, there were 323 reported arsons in Camden, which amount to almost one per police officer, three times higher than the average for the major urban cities. Due to such a high crime rate, the Camden police requested the help of New Jersey State police to crack down on drug dealing and violence at the end of 1995 (LEN, 1996).

The serious economic, social, and crime problems in the city of Camden were coupled with strong public criticisms of police corruption and mismanagement. Against this backdrop, the New Jersey state administration and the Camden city administration agreed to conduct an audit of the Camden Police Department during the last quarter of 1995 and the first quarter of 1996 to identify problems damaging police effectiveness and efficiency and suggest methods to address them. The audit was made possible by the New Jersey Local Government Budget Review Program created by the New Jersey state to help local governments find savings, improve efficiency, and reduce costs. The Local Government Budget Review Program combined expertise of professionals from several state departments such as the Department of Treasury, Community Affairs and Education, and Department of Law and Public Safety and provided the police with an auditing service at no cost by the state. In order for the police to participate in the program, the majority of elected officials in the city must request the help of the audit team through a resolution because the local government must agree to make all personnel and records available to the state audit team, and agree to an open public presentation and discussion of the audit team's findings and recommendations.

The review and dialogue between Camden police officials and the audit team in the audit process were designed to produce significant insight into what factors were driving the costs of the police department and provide the necessary tools to improve police efficiency and effectiveness. In essence, the audit was a systematic examination of the

Camden Police Department with the goal to determine the extent to which the police policies, practices, relationship with their social and political environment, and general performance were responsive to both current police industry standards and needs of the community, as well as the extent to which members of the department were properly accountable for adhering to constitutional and legal standards of performance. The final audit report, containing seventy-five recommendations for the Camden Police, was released in March 1996.

Audit Recommendations

The audit recommendations made by the state audit team and later accepted by the Camden police can be summarized under four general categories, i.e., organizational structure, patrol and patrol-related operations, serious police and crime problems, and administrative issues. In order to produce these recommendations, the audit team physically visited the department, observed the work procedures and operations, and interviewed selected department personnel. The auditors reviewed the scope of services currently provided by the police and audited data and documents from various functional units. They examined also previous audit and independent reports and annual financial statements and analyzed the geographic and demographic characteristics and criminal activities in the city over the past ten years. The audit team members reported that information they received from the Camden police was often incomplete and inconsistent. Such a condition, they believed, made it difficult to determine the current status of the organization and impeded efforts at planning.

The audit team used the core police functions identified in the New Jersey Law Enforcement Study Commission Report (1992) and some basic principles of organizational structure for law enforcement as guidelines in developing recommendations for police organizational structure. The core functions identified by the New Jersey Law Enforcement Study Commission (1992) are primary patrol, initial response to all calls for law enforcement service, arrest fingerprinting and processing, and criminal investigation. The basic principles of organizational structure in law enforcement the audit team relied upon in developing the recommended table of organization are that every police agency must be structured according to functions to provide clear lines of authority and establish accountability; personnel should be assigned to functions according to demonstrated need and be responsible to just one supervisor; functions that can be performed by nonsworn personnel should be staffed by qualified nonsworn employees; and nontraditional or highly specialized functions should be established only if a demonstrated, ongoing need exists.

The recommendations concerning police organizational structure involve the Special Operations Unit, Command Bureau, District Substations, Investigative Division, and Internal Affairs Bureau. The purposes of these recommendations were to make these programs or functions more efficient, increase their accountability, ensure their compliance with policies, avoid their fragmentation, and save financial and human resources. For example, to increase program efficiency, it was recommended that the department discontinue the Special Operations Division, which included the Tactical Force, the Special Operations Unit, the Traffic Section, and the Mounted Patrol Unit. Instead, the police should establish a tactical patrol section to focus on specific problems within a limited geographical area. It was recommended that the use of district substations as the base for patrol operations should be discontinued and all patrol operations should be centralized at the police headquarters. Selected substations or mini-stations should be used as staging areas for community policing officers only. To increase accountability, the department should assign five captains to serve in the Command Bureau on evening and night shifts, weekends and holidays, who would be responsible for all police operations in the city on their watch. To ensure compliance with policies, the department should immediately adopt the New Jersey Attorney General's internal affairs policy and procedures and the investigative procedures included therein. The operations of the Internal Affairs Bureau should be detailed in a written policy, which ensures fair and objective treatment of all reports of officer misconduct. To avoid the unnecessary fragmentation among a number of units in the Investigative, Patrol, and Service Division, the audit team recommended that the Investigative Division consist of three bureaus, i.e., the Detective Bureau, Juvenile Services Bureau, and the Narcotics Bureau. All basic uniformed police services should be handled within an Operations Division. School patrol duties should be part of the youth services function. Support services should be the responsibility of the Services Division commanded by a deputy chief. To save financial and human resources, the use of the title "Bureau Commander" and additional compensation should be discontinued.

The recommendations related to patrol involve the number of patrol officers, patrol workload analysis, patrol officer hiring and training, patrol fleet maintenance, telephone reporting section, and alternatives for securing prisoners. The purposes of these recommendations are to increase the number of patrol officers on the street, progress to the level of proactive response time, increase patrol area coverage, accomplish proportionality in patrol scheduling, ensure availability of patrol vehicles, and return patrol officers to responding to calls for service as soon as possible. The objective of patrol-related recommendations is to increase proactive patrol time by 25 percent. To do so, the audit team recommended that the Camden police increase the number of police officers to be primary responders to calls for service. The department should make the Tactical Force, the Special Operations Unit, the Traffic Section, and the Mounted Patrol Unit available for dispatch to calls for service. The number of patrol officers, tactical force officers, and community policing officers should also be increased or made available during weekends.

In order to progress to the level of proactive response time, the police should conduct regular workload analyses as a method to determine work hours and number of patrol officers assigned to each district. Ideally, officers should be deployed proportionately to meet the workload distribution. Based on a preliminary workload analysis by the audit team, the proportionate distribution of patrol officers would result in 31 additional officers scheduled for duty as first responders to calls for service. This represents a 22 percent increase over the current number of officers scheduled for first responder duties. Based on workload analyses, the department should determine work hours and days that best meet the community needs, develop schedule adjustments to provide greater coverage for those hours and days, retain the prerogative of the Camden police management to set work hours and shift schedules, and implement the recommended distribution of officers on each platoon by district.

In addition, the auditors recommended that the department train new patrol officers, develop a human resource plan to guide police recruitment efforts for filling vacancies and replacements, and reduce the time associated with filling these positions. This human resource plan can be developed in coordination with the Civil Service Department of the city. In order to take advantage of available staffing of the Patrol Operations Division, the police should ensure the availability of a fleet of patrol vehicles to equip all patrol personnel working on a given shift and establish a defined maintenance or preventative maintenance program, including the establishment of computerized fleet inventory and maintenance records and a written vehicle usage policy. The department should implement an immediate review of communications procedures, undertake the development and codification of policies and procedures for the operation of the communications center, and provide a procedural manual for all personnel. The department should develop an alternative response procedure such as a telephone-reporting unit for handling calls for service that do not require the presence of a patrol unit and review its deployment practices of its special operations units. The telephone-reporting unit should be established within the Communications Division to provide the most efficient and expeditious response to the residents and allow the patrol units to devote more time and effort toward serious crime complaints and proactive patrol. The department should also develop alternatives for securing prisoners during their processing and return arresting officers to responding to calls for service as soon as possible by implementing a training program and issuance of a Special Order outlining related procedures.

The recommendations regarding patrol operations resulted from both data analyses and physical visits. The audit team analyzed the deployment of patrol officers using data from September 1, 1995 to October 15, 1995. Police workload was measured by the total calls for service from July 1, 1994 to June 30, 1995. The team conducted a one-day direct observation of patrol operations and found that the day and afternoon shifts overlapped tours of duty from 2 p.m. to 5 p.m. on that day. This overlap resulted in a full double staffing of the patrol function for the three hours, during which the personnel on the relieved shift "disappeared" from the communications operators' screen and paper tracking was used. The team also found that the officers assigned to the Special Operations Unit, Traffic Section, School Patrol, and Mounted Unit did not leave their duty assignments routinely to answer calls for service.

The recommendations regarding serious police and crime problems cover false alarms, domestic violence, and drugs. These problems tend to drain substantial amount of police resources. For example, it was estimated that responding to false alarms cost the city more than 6,100 officer hours or 5.4 percent of total consumed officer time annually, amounting to a loss of hours equivalent to those of five full-time patrol officers. The audit team believed that if the police were able to reduce these problems, they would be in a position to devote more resources to crime prevention and deterrent patrol and eventually crime reduction. The recommendations for addressing the large number of false alarms include sanctions and fines against flagrant violators of the city's false alarm ordinance.

The department should also examine alternatives to handling domestic violence workload. A domestic violence response team consisting of municipal officers, county sheriff's officers, and trained civilians should be established to have a stronger focus on this issue. A police liaison should be appointed to work with the municipal prosecutor on plea bargaining in order to process domestic violence cases more efficiently. The department should conduct a specific analysis of the locations, times, patterns, and causes of domestic violence so more effective operations can be developed in dealing with domestic violence. A sergeant should be assigned to full-time domestic violence response duties, who in the meantime should analyze related New Jersey State Division of Criminal Justice programs and coordinate a domestic violence response team consisting of sheriff's officers, community policing officers, social workers, family counselors, and volunteers to reduce the hours patrol officers spend on this issue.

The Narcotics Bureau should direct emphasis on street-level narcotics investigations, including arresting purchasers and dealers. Personnel assigned to this bureau should work on a schedule dictated by their ongoing investigative activities. When necessary, the bureau should utilize Tactical Patrol Section personnel to assist in street sweeps, sting operations, and other operational activities. Personnel assigned to federal drug enforcement agencies should be the responsibility of the lieutenant assigned to this bureau for managerial and coordination purposes. The bureau should maintain a close liaison with county and other law enforcement agencies with similar investigative responsibilities for intelligence exchange and coordination of efforts where appropriate. The department should regularly monitor its commitment to specialized task forces outside the agency. While these task forces can be successful in dealing with specifically defined problems and enhancing the resources of the investigative section, the police should be assured that the emphasis of the task forces' activities is in and around the city of Camden.

To deal with false alarms, domestic violence, and drug problems effectively, the police should develop concrete and specific policies to make community policing a long-term, department-wide policing strategy with or without outside grant supports. How different bureaus, sections, and units cooperate and work together under the principle of prevention and problem-solving should be further specified to achieve the objective of crime prevention and lowering the crime rate in Camden. Available and effective community-policing tactics in use in other departments should be seriously considered. Police officers should shift from the role of specialists to that of generalists and be given more autonomy and accountability in performing different duties such as criminal and accident investigation, problem solving, crime prevention, and community education. All city government officials should be involved in building a safer community because many police operations and problem-solving measures require the support and cooperation of other city agencies. There should also be more involvement of the media in publicizing the police efforts in community crime prevention. More use of volunteers should be made at police substations and mini-stations.

Various recommendations were made concerning administrative and managerial issues of the police. These include the communications center, solvability factors, sick leave abuse, financial transactions, body armor, civilianization, training, benefits, and budget savings. The purposes of these recommendations are to formalize police procedures, increase police supervision, tighten police disciplines, increase officer safety, civilianize staff function, raise staff qualifications, increase police automation, standardize purchasing and record keeping, and reduce cost. For example, to formalize police procedures, it was recommended that the department implement an immediate review of communications procedures, undertake the development and codification of policies and procedures for the operation of the communications center, and provide a procedure manual for all communications personnel. The department should reevaluate its solvability factor policy and establish appropriate criteria as the standard operating procedure, which should provide oversight of the classification process and the sign-off by an appropriate commander when an assigned case that has not been cleared by an arrest is to be closed. Written policies should also be established for selection of officers to attend special training and for key assignments. All training should be recorded and all training records should be consolidated in one location. To increase supervision, the Communications Center should be redesigned to provide the supervising sergeant visible access to all positions. To increase officer safety, the department should consider issuing body armor to all officers as part of their standard duty equipment. To civilianize the staff function, civilians should be hired to conduct clerical duties, staff communications office, dispatch emergency calls, and serve as computer operators to relieve the police officers. To tighten disciplines, the department should develop a procedure for formal staff inspections. Sick time should be closely monitored and officers that abuse sick leave should be penalized.

Process Evaluation

Process evaluation of the Camden police audit was conducted by an outside evaluator covering roughly a six-month period after the audit report was presented to the police. The police first discussed the audit recommendations among themselves and later with city officials, civilian representatives, and university faculty. The recommendations were embellished and prioritized during these discussions and the schedules for implementing them were planned. The process evaluation addressed the audit implementation process by which immediate and intermediate objectives were achieved. The elements related to the process include audit program development, organizational design, patrol deployment, problem-solving activities, and changes in administrative and financial policies. The audit implementation process was evaluated with the use of multiple data sources, including participant observations, documentary analyses, and personal interviews.

The implementation of the Camden police audit involved participants from both inside and outside the Camden Police Department and the Camden city administration. The key players among insiders included the management team appointed by the chief of police, which consisted of police executives and bargaining unit officials and was charged with the responsibility to carry out the audit recommendations. The key players among outsiders included the state audit team set up by the New Jersey state government and the Camden Budget Review and Quality Management Task Force appointed by the mayor of Camden. To address the Camden police audit specifically, the Task Force created a public safety subcommittee consisting of police executives, police union leaders, community representatives, city council members, and an academic. The involvement of both insiders and outsiders neutralized the partisan, race, and class issues, real or perceived, that would arise if one or the other side had taken control over the audit and its implementation process. The collaborative approach to the audit program increased both sides' ownership of the final product.

The management team and the public safety subcommittee deliberated and reached consensus on most of the audit recommendations. They decided that the Camden police should utilize the hoshin planning for prioritizing the recommendations. Hoshin planning is a planning and management system that focuses and aligns the organization to achieve breakthroughs for its customers. Six key factors contribute to successful hoshin planning, i.e., ability to prioritize, a commitment to customers, deployment of the organization's focus, collective wisdom to develop the plan, tools and techniques, and ongoing evaluation of progress (Melum & Collett, 1995). Combining this method with total quality management techniques, the police separated the recommendations into three categories: those in need of financial assistance, those not requiring financial assistance, and those compatible with the goals and objectives of the department's mission statement. Determining that providing the maximum number of officers for emergency response was the highest priority, the police set immediate objectives to implement recommendations related to patrol deployment, overall response time, workload analysis, and serious crime problems. As a result of their deliberations, the police assigned a time frame for action for each recommendation in one of four categories: immediate within 45 days, short-term within 90 days, intermediate from 90 days to 6 months, and long-range from 6 months to 1 year. The police management team and the public safety subcommittee also reached consensus on tracking and monitoring police activities related to implementing the recommendations. As a result, the following activities and changes had taken place during the year after the audit was completed.

First, the department reorganized its internal structure and increased its hierarchical efficiency to conform to recommendations related to police organizational structure. The Special Operations Division and the Tactical Force function were integrated into the Patrol Bureau. The positions of bureau commanders and duty officers were eliminated, the number of captains and lieutenants reduced, and the title of adjutant was changed to administrative assistant. The chief appointed two inspectors to take charge of line and staff functions. The line inspector was responsible for commanding all police operations including the Patrol Division. The Patrol Division was put under the command of two captains who reported directly to the line inspector; one captain was in charge of the north side of the city, the other the south side, as the city was being divided into two police divisions. The north division housed both the first and third district at one location; the south houses the second and fourth district. Every officer working in these districts was accountable to the captains.

Second, more police officers were made available to respond to initial calls for service, following patrol-related recommendations. The Traffic Bureau, Special Operations, and the Tactical Force were assigned to districts as first responders. The Traffic Bureau's duties were expanded to include handling calls for services. Although patrol officers' work hours were determined during union negotiations and could not be immediately changed according to the audit recommendations, patrol hours were adjusted for officers in the Traffic Bureau, Special Operations Division, and Community Policing Unit. Eighteen community policing officers provided by the Partnership Grant from the state of New Jersey for the third district were placed in first responder positions after their grant period ended. The department analyzed the total calls for services, changed the overlapping period between tours of duty, and defined eleven demographic areas as "cutback beats." The fifteen primary patrol beats were supplemented with these cutback beats bringing the total to twenty-six defined areas of patrol service. A series of other measures were implemented to increase patrol efficiency and save patrol officer time such as advanced communication linkage, development of the telephone complaint system, walk-in complaint program, secured holding areas for prisoners, and booking assistance. Patrol officers were trained on the booking process to better assist the desk sergeants.

In order to ensure smooth patrol operations, the department took immediate action to address the fleet management problem. The Patrol Fleet Management Unit was expanded and a computer was placed in Property Management for keeping all records of police vehicles and tracking repairs. In February 1996, the 1992 Chevrolets were taken out of service while a new fleet of 25 vehicles were put in service. The 1994 Fords were used as backups or for the cutback beats when the 1996 vehicles went into service. Two full-time mechanics were employed to make repairs on the vehicles older than two years.

Third, the department took a series of measures to reduce false alarms, domestic violence, and drug-related crimes, following recommendations related to serious police problems. An aggressive problem-oriented approach was implemented to deter and prevent false alarms. A lieutenant was assigned to oversee the false alarm program and one officer from each of the four community-oriented policing districts and one detective from the Crime Prevention Unit participated in the program. The problem-oriented approach to dealing with false alarms included analysis of alarm calls, public education, distributions of fliers of related city ordinance, repeated offender focus, and mandated installation of better alarm systems. A computer printout of all alarms during 1995 was produced to assist the police in identifying excessive alarm locations.

Community police officers were given the responsibility for identifying the residences or businesses with excessive false alarms. These officers would visit the false alarm locations and inspect the alarm systems to determine the reasons behind the excessive number of alarms. They would give the residents and/or merchants a copy of the city ordinance at the time of visit and solicit their cooperation in resolving the large number of false alarms. The officers also coordinated with the residents and/or businesses and the alarm companies to resolve false alarms. If residents and/or merchants contacted by the police for excessive false alarms continued to have the problem, the officers assigned would issue summonses for violations of the city ordinance.

The police expanded the Domestic Violence Unit and the Vice Unit. A detective sergeant was placed in charge of coordinating domestic violence incidents and training was provided to domestic violence responders. The Domestic Violence Unit now had the sole responsibility for responding to and handling domestic violence calls. A

sergeant was assigned to full-time domestic violence duties, who analyzed related New Jersey State Division of Criminal Justice programs
and coordinated a domestic violence response team consisting of sheriff's officers, community policing officers, social workers, family counselors, and volunteers to reduce the hours patrol officers spent on this
problem. In the area of drug offenses, the police believed that there
were approximately 200 drug locations throughout the city that presented a pattern of drug-related crime and violence. In response to this
continual problem that defied efforts to maintain neighborhood sta-
bility and attract new businesses, the police expanded the Vice Unit
from six to eighteen officers. The vice officers were divided into four
sections with two officers accountable in each district for targeting
high-intensity drug trafficking areas.

Fourth, the department implemented various measures to address its
administrative issues. The training and education program was expanded; all newly promoted supervisors and many police officers received
training after the audit was completed. The department developed a
new human resource plan in collaboration with the City Department of
Personnel. Following the Department of Personnel policies, the police
changed the procedures and written directives concerning the use of
sick time. Counsel, charge, written reprimand, and suspension were
used in controlling sick-time abuse and all commanders were made
responsible for the enforcement of the sick-time policy within their command. Police administrative office hours were lengthened until 6 p.m.
for all services. More civilians were hired for staff functions. To reduce
the number of school crossing guards, the department contacted each
elementary school to determine if the children left school at lunch time.
The police were able to identify 30 posts that did not require a school
crossing guard during the lunch-time period.

Outcome Evaluation

The public safety subcommittee had suggested during the audit
report deliberation that an outcome evaluation be conducted to evaluate the internal and external effects of the audit program. Such an
evaluation would help the police determine the usefulness of the audit
recommendations and develop better policies for their future operations. The outcome evaluation involves examining whether the police
accomplished the audit program objectives and what effects the

accomplishment had on police performance and crime rates. Outcome variables examined include management overheads, command responsibilities, and matching of resources with demands. More specifically, they involve cost comparisons, patrol manpower level, workload distribution, use of sick days, arrest statistics, radio assignment, and crime rate. Because an outcome evaluation involves minimally a pretest before and a posttest after the implementation of the recommendations, the evaluator must determine the kinds of pre and posttest data that should be collected for comparisons. The data selected eventually for comparisons included the number of patrol officers on the street, the number of false alarms, and the percentages of workload distribution among various units before and after the implementation of the audit recommendations. The pre and posttest comparisons allowed the police to assess if any changes had occurred as a result of the audit program.

Over 90 percent of the audit recommendations were implemented as planned during the two years after the audit was completed. The implementation produced positive internal effects in all four recommended areas. First, the police organizational structure was redefined and promoted accountability. Limited to the numbers of existing ranks, the department was restructured in close proximity to what was recommended in the audit report. In terms of cost savings, the department saved $530,319 by reducing ranks (see Table 1). The elimination of five rotating captains offset the cost of two inspectors' salaries. Shift differential savings from taking five captains out of rotation resulted in additional annual savings of $25,000. The recommended manpower strength of 377, however, was not accomplished. The department manpower strength was 349 at the time when the audit was completed and was down to 331 a year and a half later after the police completed implementing most of the recommendations because the city government was unable to provide funding for the appointment of new officers as well as promotions, the city administrator's office was unable to change its officer certification policy and raise certification rate to allow the police to hire more officers, and the police department experienced a number of retirements during the two years after the audit. It is important to note that although the department realized substantial savings by elimination of certain ranks, the need for new officers would have offset some of these savings.

Table 1.
POST-AUDIT FINANCIAL SAVINGS WITH RANK LEVELS.

Rank	Amount
Bureau Commander 2 to 0	– $143,956.00
Inspector 1 to 2	+ $ 75,500.00
Captain 11 to 5	– $431,556.00
Lieutenant 23 to 22	– $ 64,666.00
Sergeant 55 to 56	+ $ 59,359.00
Shift Differential Savings	– $ 25,000.00
Total Savings	– $530,319.00

Two of the recommendations related to police organizational structure were either partially or not implemented. The Mounted Patrol Unit was disbanded as a unit according to the audit recommendation, but mounted patrol activities remained a part of patrol operations. Three mounted patrol officers were reassigned to patrol duties and the remaining sergeant and one officer were moved to the community policing unit. The mounted patrol activities remained ongoing because the department had received external funding and facility support for this program. Also, according to the police, mounted patrol provided the department with an added dimension of horse patrol, which had been received positively by the public and quite a success. The recommendation that traffic duties related to fatal accident investigations be transferred to the Investigative Division was not adopted because the police believed that the accident investigation function would be better served in its current structure as part of the Traffic Bureau. The accident investigator had the experience of investigating numerous fatal accidents and this knowledge/expertise being vitally important, transferring this function to various investigative officers would not be conducive to accurate reporting.

Second, in patrol operations, the police answered 290 radio calls on average daily. Uniform patrol handled 222 of the calls or 75.6 percent, tactical patrol 17 of the calls or 5.8 percent, community police 12 calls or 4.2 percent, Detective Bureau 12 calls or 4.2 percent, Traffic Bureau 3 calls or 1.1 percent, and district houses 4 calls or 1.4 percent. This was a result of police efforts in increasing the number of officers as first responders and improving response time. The police exceeded the objective of increasing proactive patrol time by 25 percent as 29.9 percent more police officers were made available to respond to calls for service. A comparison of officer distribution and workload (see Table 2) indicates that approximately 16.7 percent of the workload was handled by the district patrol officers and 7.1 percent by special operations officers during evening hours. This was an improvement compared to the audit finding of 17.2 percent and 1.8 percent respectively. During the day shift, the district patrol officers handled 17.4 percent of the calls for service while special operations handled 17.4 percent of the calls also. This was a dramatic improvement compared to the audit finding that 23.8 percent of the calls were handled by the patrol districts and only 2.8 percent by special operations officers.

Third, in the area of serious police and crime problems, the police were able to lower the number of false alarm calls, reduce the number of domestic violence calls, and increase drug-related arrests. Pre- and post-audit comparison of burglar alarms indicated that although burglar alarms increased by 6.3 percent, the bank alarms decreased by 64.1 percent. Domestic violence dropped by 18.5 percent. The Vice Unit had a significant impact not only on drug-related arrests but arrest rates in general. As Table 3 indicates, total arrests decreased by 5.3 percent from 1995 to 1996 and went up by 17.8 percent from 1996 to 1997. Total arrests also increased by 11.5 percent when the total numbers between 1995 and 1997 are compared. The decrease in arrests in 1996 was consistent with the lower crime rates in Camden in

Table 2.
PRE- AND POST-AUDIT COMPARISON OF
OFFICER DISTRIBUTION AND WORKLOAD.

	District Patrol	*Special Operations*	*Total*
Before the Audit			45.6%
Evening	17.2%	1.8%	
Day	23.8%	2.8%	
After the Audit			58.6%
Evening	16.7%	7.1%	
Day	17.4%	17.4%	

Source: Camden Police Research and Development Unit, 1997.

Table 3.
COMPARISON OF TOTAL ARRESTS: 1995, 1996, 1997.

	Year			% Change		
	1995	1996	1997	95–96	96–97	95–97
Total Arrests	6,841	6,477	7,630	–5.3	+17.8	+11.5

Source: Camden Police Research and Development Unit, 1998.

that year. The increase in 1997 reflected to a large extent the expansion of the Vice Unit, which was completed at the end of 1996 and became fully operational in 1997. According to the police records, the Vice Unit more than doubled the number of arrests they made in 1997. The quality of these arrests also increased as the police were able to arrest not only street dealers but also drug suppliers.

Lastly, the police addressed a series of administrative and support issues according to related audit recommendations. Operations of the Training and Education Unit were expanded and officer productivity in these units was increased. Accountability of forfeiture funding was enhanced as funds were reconciled monthly with the City Finance Department. Positive change had also occurred in the total number of sick days. Although there was a 6.1 percent increase in 1996 in the total number of sick days, which could be a result of the higher number of total police employees and retirements in that year, there was a reduction of 8.1 percent and 2.4 percent respectively when the percentage of total sick days between 1996 and 1997 and between 1995 and 1997 are compared (see Table 4). In addition, overtime expenditures were monitored more closely to ensure compliance with the operational fiscal budget. The school crossing guards were reduced

Table 4.
SICK DAYS: 1995, 1996, 1997.

	Year			% Change		
	1995	1996	1997	95–96	96–97	95–97
Totals	3,341	3,548	3,258	+6.1	–8.1	–2.4

Source: Camden Police Research and Development Unit, 1998.

from 141 to 121. With the elimination of twenty unnecessary guard posts, $240,000 savings were realized for the school year.

Not all cited financial items in the police audit report, however, have validity and not all dollar amounts can be directly linked to accomplished items. It is necessary sometimes to increase expenditure in order to increase efficiency in the long run. Financial assistance and addition of new personnel, for instance, were required to complete the civilianization programs recommended in the audit. The connection of all computer terminals in the substations to the main computer system was required to enhance the communication system. There were also items not mentioned in the audit report but should be addressed by the police. For example, the department should give serious consideration to assigning a court liaison officer for giving reoccurring testimonies in the Camden Municipal Court in order to reduce cost.

An overview of these internal audit outcomes in the four recommended areas (i.e., police organizational structure, patrol operations, serious problems, and administrative issues) indicates that overall measurable improvements in police performances had occurred after the audit was completed. Most significantly, the police were able to reduce cost, increase accountability, strengthen patrol manpower, improve workload distribution, reduce sick days, and improve arrest statistics. While these accomplishments can be used to measure police efforts in enhancing their internal management, to what extent can they be used to explain the external effects on crimes and public safety is subject to discussion.

Neither the auditors nor the police explicitly spelled out the intended or hypothesized effects of implementing the audit recommendations on crime and public safety. No external goals were set for the police to attain. This creates difficulty in evaluating the external impact of the audit program. It can be argued, however, that the overall goal of changing police organizational structure, operations, programs, and administrative functions is to lower the crime rates and improve public safety. This goal had not been made explicit, but it was clearly implied. It is with this understanding that the audit program's effect on crime rates is discussed here. As described earlier, the police had successfully implemented a series of programs to target serious crime and police problems in Camden according to the audit recommendations. Their endeavors in beefing up patrol and implementing a more proactive patrol program may have deterred certain criminal activities. The program to reduce false alarms and the joint effort of the Domestic Violence Response Team may have had an effect on reducing these problems as well.

Major crime categories (i.e., murder, rape, robbery, aggravated assault, burglary, theft, auto theft, and arson) showed a total reduction of 24.9 percent in 1996 and 25.3 percent in 1997 (see Table 5) when crime rates between 1995 and later years are compared. Major calls for service in 1997 decreased by 15.3 percent compared to the rate in 1995 (see Table 6). One area that had contributed to the decrease of calls was in the city's Housing and Urban Development communities, where "man-with-a-gun type of calls" was reduced by 28 percent on average. Roosevelt Manor experienced a 57 percent reduction of calls from 42 calls in 1995 to 18 in 1996; Branch Village had a 46 percent reduction from 37 to 20; Ablett Village dropped 11 percent from 65 to 58; the Westfield Acres dropped 53 percent from 17 to 8; and McGuire Gardens dropped 28 percent from 126 to 91. The remaining development of Chelton Terrace had a slight increase of 9 percent from 35 to 38.

The effects of the audit program on crimes can be further examined by looking at crime rates in similar cities and surrounding areas. The reduction of crime in other urban centers in New Jersey such as Trenton, Paterson, and Elizabeth was not as great as that in Camden

Table 5.
CRIME RATES: 1995, 1996, 1997.

| | | Year | | | % Change | |
Category	1995	1996	1997	95–96	96–97	95–97
Murder	58	28	40	–51.7	+42.8	–31.0
Rape	89	102	96	+14.6	–5.8	+7.8
Robbery	1,593	1,280	1,110	–19.7	–13.2	+30.3
Agg. Assault	1,486	1,188	1,161	–20.5	–2.2	–21.8
Burglary	3,199	2,329	2,452	–27.2	+5.2	–23.3
Theft	3,780	2,918	2,772	–22.8	–5.0	–26.6
Auto Theft	2,014	1,342	1,493	–33.3	+11.2	–25.8
Arson	367	262	277	–28.6	+5.7	–24.5
Totals	12,586	9,449	9,401	–24.9	–0.5	–25.3

Source: Camden Police Research and Development Unit, 1998.

Table 6.
COMPARISON OF TOTAL ARRESTS: 1995, 1996, 1997.

Assignment	Year			% Change		
	1995	*1996*	*1997*	*95–96*	*96–97*	*95–97*
Burglar Alarms	12.200	13,041	12,974	+6.8	−0.5	+6.3
Domestic Violence	16,691	14,342	13,597	−14.0	−5.2	−18.5
Gun Calls	5,293	3,383	3,205	−36.0	−5.2	−39.4
Disturbances	13,381	13,909	12,174	+3.9	−12.4	−9.0
Crime in Progress	4,346	2,894	2,175	−33.4	−24.8	−49.9
Bank Alarms	346	155	124	−55.2	−20.0	−64.1
Totals	12,586	9,449	9,401	−24.9	−0.5	−25.3

Source: Camden Police Research and Development Unit, 1998.

during the period when the audit recommendations were implemented. The crime rates not only decreased in Camden but also in all surrounding towns such as Pennsauken, Merchantville, Collingswood, Woodlynne, Audubon Park, Oaldyn, and Gloucester City per 1,000 people. The crime rates in suburban townships some distance away from Camden including Cherry Hill, Moorestown, Burlington Township, Mount Laurel, West Deptford, Deptford, and Washington Township did not see any decrease per 1,000 people (Division of State Police, 1997). These crime data indicate that the Camden police efforts in implementing the audit recommendations may have produced not only an effect on the crime rates in the city but also a diffusion of benefits to the immediately surrounding areas. The suburban townships some distance away from Camden did not observe any decrease in crime rates perhaps because their distance from Camden made them less affected and their own demographic and policing conditions were relatively stable.

Any causality between a police audit program and a lower crime rate must be interpreted with caution, however, especially when reducing overall crime rates was not identified as a goal. The Camden police audit examined the entire department without targeting any specific impact variables such as crime rates and community satisfaction. Camden police activities in response to the audit were focused on improving internal management, which resulted in more efficient police operations, but their accomplishments should not be used to explain the lower crime rates directly. Police efforts in increasing their effi-

ciency are simply not equivalent to their efforts in solving crime problems (Bayley, 1993) and the effects on crime rates could not be as-
cribed to a single simple change (Ekblom & Pease, 1995). Furthermore, research has suggested that changes in police activities not only
have a limited effect on the reported crime rate, but in certain circumstances, police sensitivity in responding to crimes such as rape,
child abuse, and racial attacks may increase the number of such crimes
reported (Audit Commission, 1990).

A variety of factors other than the efforts of the Camden police
such as multi-agency operations, socioeconomic improvement, crime
fluctuation, weather conditions, and curfew laws could have affected
the crime rate in Camden. Multi-law enforcement agency operations
played a significant role in Camden during the period when the audit
recommendations were implemented. The Camden Initiative, a program that included the New Jersey State Police, County Prosecutor,
DEA, and other agencies, started its operations in January 1996. Although this initiative terminated its visible activities to a large degree
by June 1996, selected programs such as the Joint Domestic Violence
Response Team remained ongoing. The State Police also expanded
their duties at the request of Camden police to provide additional coverage of incidents requiring a swift response time. Because Camden is
an extremely poor city, any improvement in its socioeconomic conditions such as employment, housing, and general services may have a
greater effect on its crime rate than on crime rates of more affluent
suburban townships. Regression to the mean was another factor as the
crime rate in 1996 might have reverted to its average, considering that
1995 was a year of a particularly high crime rate for the city. Regression to the mean is related to the problem of fluctuation in detecting change and estimating effect. Fluctuation tends to be great when
numbers are small (Ekblom et al., 1995). In a city like Camden,
although there are disproportionate numbers of major crimes, the
numbers of these crimes are relatively small. The severe weather conditions (e.g., a blizzard) during the winter of 1996 could be another
possibility that had affected deviant behaviors during the first quarter
of the year. Lastly, the curfew laws of 1996 might have played a significant role in reducing youth crimes in the city.

SUMMARY

The Camden police audit was conducted by the New Jersey State Department of Public Safety in late 1995 and early 1996 to identify problems that were damaging police efficiency and effectiveness and suggest methods for addressing them. The result of the audit was a list of seventy-five recommendations contained in the police audit report, which are concerned with four categories of police issues, i.e., organizational structure, patrol operations, serious police and crime problems, and administrative services. The recommendations concerning police organizational structure involve Special Operations, Command Bureau, District Substations, Investigative Division, and Internal Affairs. The purposes of these recommendations were to make these programs or functions more efficient, increase accountability, ensure compliance, avoid fragmentation, and save financial and human resources. Recommendations related to patrol operations involve the number of patrol officers, workload analysis, patrol officer hiring and training, patrol fleet maintenance, communications, and alternatives for securing prisoners. These recommendations were driven by the need to increase the number of patrol officers on the street, progress to the level of proactive response time, increase patrol area coverage, accomplish proportionality in patrol scheduling, ensure availability of patrol vehicles, and return more patrol officers to responding to calls for service as quickly as possible. Recommendations regarding serious police and crime problems such as false alarms, domestic violence, and drugs were intended to reduce and control these problems and in the meantime decrease the amount of police resources used for responding to such problems. Recommendations concerning administrative matters are related to the Communications Center, solvability factors, sick leave abuse, financial transactions, body armor, civilianization, training, benefits, and budgets. The purpose of these recommendations was to increase the efficiency and effectiveness of support functions in the police department.

In response to these recommendations, the police reorganized its internal structure and increased its hierarchical efficiency. The Special Operations Division, the Tactical Force, and the Traffic Bureau now functioned within the Patrol Bureau. More police officers were made available to respond to initial calls for service. Patrol officers' workload was analyzed and their work hours were adjusted to better meet the needs of the community. A lieutenant was assigned to oversee the false alarm program, who worked with community police officers, detectives, and crime prevention officers to target false alarm problems. A detective sergeant was placed in charge of coordinating domestic violence incidents and managing a domestic violence response team. The Vice Unit was expanded to target high-intensity drug trafficking areas. The department implemented a series of measures to address its administrative issues and improve its staff support functions and services. The training program was expanded, a new human resource plan was developed, procedures and written directives concerning the use of sick time were changed, more civilians were hired, and unnecessary school crossing guard posts were identified.

As a result of implementing the audit recommendations, the police organizational structure was redefined and accountability was promoted. The department was structured in close proximity to that recommended by the auditors, accomplished budget savings by reducing ranks, and disbanded the Mounted Patrol as a separate unit. The uniform patrol, tactical patrol force, community police officers, Detective Bureau, Traffic Bureau, and district houses all handled calls for service; as a result, the police exceeded the objective of increasing proactive patrol time by 25 percent. The workload distribution between district patrol officers and special operations officers became more equitable. The police were able to reduce the number of false alarms in businesses, reduce domestic violence calls, and increase the number of drug-related arrests. There was a reduction in total officer sick days. And unnecessary school crossing guard posts were eliminated. Police were not, however, able to implement several recommendations that required financial assistance and personnel approval from the city or agreement with the union. These difficulties aside, the audit program proved to be a positive experience that had effected desired changes in the department and improved its ability to serve the community.

REFERENCES

Audit Commission of Local Authorities and the National Health Service in England and Wales. (1990). Effective policing–performance review in police forces. *Police Papers*, 8.

Bayley, D. H. (1993). Back from wonderland, or toward the rational use of police resources. In A. N. Doob (Ed.), *Thinking about police resources.* Toronto: University of Toronto, Center for Criminology.

Division of State Police. (1994). *Crime in New Jersey.* Trenton, NJ: State of New Jersey Division of State Police.

Division of State Police. (1997). *Crime in New Jersey.* Trenton, NJ: State of New Jersey Division of State Police.

Ekblom, P., & Pease, K. (1995). Evaluating crime prevention. In M. Tonry & D. P. Farrington (Eds.), *Building a safer society: Strategic approaches to crime prevention.* Chicago: The University of Chicago Press.

Law Enforcement News (LEN). (1996). Camden sends out for the cavalry in the form of NJ state troopers. January 31, 438, 1 & 9.

Melum, M. M., & Collett, C. (1995). *Breakthrough leadership: Achieving organizational alignment through hoshin planning.* Chicago: American Hospital Publishing.

New Jersey Law Enforcement Study Commission. (1992). *New Jersey law enforcement study commission report.* Trenton, NJ: New Jersey Division of Criminal Justice.

Riordan, K. (1996). Camden faces $11 million budget gap. *Courier-Post,* August 12, 1B & 2B.

Rouse, E. (1996). Where action is in Camden County: Cherry Hill. *The Philadelphia Inquirer,* June 23, B1 & B2.

Shralow, B. (1996). Poverty awareness forum held. *Courier-Post,* June 23.

U.S. Department of the Census. (1990). *Census of population and housing 1990.* Washington, D.C.: U.S. Government Printing Office.

Chapter 9

CONCLUSIONS

Police auditing, from theories, standards, procedures, to applications and evaluations, represents a model of planned change. This model, which is based on systematic information collected for an audit program, should prove beneficial to police organizations at all levels of government. Police departments, by following this model, can expect to enhance critical areas in their management and operations, including their organizational structure, administrative efficiencies, patrol activities, and criminal investigations. Such improvements can have a further impact on crime and public safety if such a goal is targeted explicitly by auditors. The entire process of an audit program and the outcome of implementing audit recommendations involve the basic elements of the model of planned change. This concluding chapter provides a discussion of these essential constructs as applied to police auditing.

Eight interrelated elements make up this model of planned change (see Figure 1). The first is concerned with external and internal pressures for changing the police. These pressures come primarily from two sources: a high demand for police services and declining resources for meeting that demand. They can be especially intense when a city is experiencing a high crime or incident rate while being mired in financial difficulties. As these pressures and demands become explicit, they are transformed into a political process that involves various interest groups and stakeholders. These groups and stakeholders, through conflicts and negotiations, may choose to adopt a neutral strategy for improving the police in the form of a police audit. The proposal for a police audit that affects different sectors of a city should be based on

External and Internal Pressures

Performance Gap<->Organizational Disequilibrium<->Problems

Systematic Examination/Data Collection

Innovative, Rational Decision-Making

Goals and Objectives<->Developing Solutions<->Alternatives

Sources of Resistance<->Implementing Change<->Organizational Development

Maintenance and Monitoring of Change

Outcome Evaluations

Figure 1. The Model of Planned Change through Police Auditing.

input from representatives of these areas and the decision to eventually conduct the audit should be made through compromise and agreement between them and the police.

Major stakeholders in police auditing include organizations that
provide funding and resources to the police department in question,
the state and municipal government under which the police operate,
the police themselves, the public, and local businesses. If a state government provides much of the financial resources to a local government in the form of state aides and grants, it would have an interest in
influencing the total expenditure on local government services as part
of its overall control of public spending. A municipal government that
makes overall budgetary decisions for its police department would also
have a stake in controlling its police expenditure. The police department, on the other hand, is likely to put stronger emphasis on effective
policing in response to local demands. This means they will be attract-
ed to a system that maximizes their flexibility in resource deployment
(Ingram, 1990). The public and the local business community represent a hybrid of interests between the state/municipal government and
the police. Local residents and businesses like to see their tax dollars
used economically and efficiently and demand a safer living and business environment in the meantime.

The different pressures from various stakeholders influence police auditors' agendas and related activities. Politicians that appoint and direct auditors often determine what auditors do or do not do. Effective auditors should have a proper vision of police accountability, good direction from political leaders, thorough understanding of what it takes to achieve their goals, good grasp of the role they can play in the auditing process, and ready cooperation of the chief of police or sheriff whose departments they are about to audit (Walker, 2005).

The second element, performance gaps and associated agency problems, usually result from external and internal pressures and can further develop into organizational disequilibrium. There are two types of performance gaps, a general one that influences a major police division or various police functions or an entire agency and a specialized one that affects a specific police unit or section or program only. A general performance gap influencing an entire police department could occur when the police are unable to meet the service demand in their jurisdiction. A specialized performance gap affecting a specific police function could happen when the communications unit is insufficiently trained in using advanced computer systems. Performance gaps often transpire in the forms of both low productivity and low morale (March & Simon, 1958) caused by confusing policies, unclear procedures, and insufficient training. These problems must be made known to police administrators to allow the police audit and the change process to begin. If not, police organizations may simply alter symbols and dress windows to placate the pressure groups (Klofas et al., 1990). Police executives that are convinced that a performance gap exists in their agency will be more likely to request an audit and more predisposed toward reorganizing their department and streamlining their operations.

The third element, systematic examination and data collection, is essential for police auditing because it provides the basis for an objective analysis of the police department by describing accurately the current conditions of the police as related to audit issues such as budgetary control, policy compliance, administrative services, organizational structure, police operations, and crime problems. Collection and examination of data in police auditing, however, are rarely viewed equitable by all stakeholders. Police officials may question the methods used in collecting and examining the data. They may dispute why certain data that reflect negatively on them are examined while other data that project a more positive image of them are ignored, why only certain officials are interviewed while others are not, why a selective sample is used rather than a randomized survey of the entire department, and why an unstructured rather than structured questionnaire is used in obtaining the information. The auditors, on the other hand, may be accustomed to gathering information in ways unfamiliar to the police officials. They may find it justifiable to interview only low-ranking officers rather than those in decision-making positions and use unstructured instead of structured questionnaires for interviews. The fact of the matter is that auditing is by its very nature a critical process because its purpose is to bring about corrections and improvements (Brown et al., 1982).

Being critical is apparently not the same as ensuring a sophisticated and systematic data collection process. In order to gather quality information, auditors should follow sound research methods. They should familiarize themselves first with the audited agency to prevent misunderstandings that may occur in their communications with the police. They then must demonstrate professional ethics and an unbiased attitude toward the audited organization in all their data collection activities. Certain temptations often distract the auditors from maintaining a high professional standard such as deciding prematurely that police should use a particular technique whether it is essential to the analysis or not, becoming overly eager about the possibility of bringing about change, and providing findings sought by those who order the audit or preconceived by auditors themselves (Brown et al., 1982). Auditors must guard against such leanings and act professionally in order to secure police cooperation and obtain accurate data. Preconceived ideas about the existence of misconduct or low performance would result in unsophisticated and incorrect data that may lead to recommendations that are confusing or difficult to implement or ask the police to do what they are already doing.

Fourth, police auditing involves innovative, rational decision-making, which requires that police executives charged with the responsibility to implement audit recommendations deliberate and plan their implementation activities. In this process, the police officials should move away from traditional assumptions about police work and base their decisions on empirical research and creative thinking. They should regard the audit as an excellent opportunity to be innovative and rational in providing police services, look at the issues they face from a comprehensive perspective, and devise creative strategies to confront them. The police can, for example, conduct workload analysis and schedule overlapping shifts during high-crime hours to increase their strength during those hours without hiring more officers (Poole, 1980).

Fifth, innovative, rational decision-making is interrelated to development of solutions, setting objectives and goals, and searching for alternatives. Planned change resulting from a police audit requires that police executives manage their organizations by goals and objectives (Audit Commission, 1990). To develop goals and objectives, the city government and the police department should discuss first the audit recommendations they have received from the auditors with participation of various interest groups, stakeholders, and experts such as state senators, assembly members, city officials, police officers, community representatives, and academicians. These discussions are essential because an audit is often focused on problems and organizational maladaptation but is short on specific solutions (Mackenzie, 1986). With these deliberations, the police officials will be in a better position to transform audit recommendations into goals and objectives. The audit thus paves the way for the police to develop short- and long-range strategies and even a three-to-five-year operational plan. The police should also consider alternatives other than the solutions they have developed and decided to implement in case their original plans do not pan out. Alternative approaches should incorporate an orientation toward flexibility, which means that police officers may work as generalists rather than specialists and that hierarchical statuses and prerogatives may shift.

Participation of members from outside the police organization in developing audit solutions may complicate the implementation process, but is critical for reaching audit objectives and goals because outside members are usually the beneficiaries of a police audit and the ultimate goal of the audit is to create a safe living and business environment for local residents and merchants. When community representatives are engaged in audit deliberations, they often demand that focus be put on addressing the needs and concerns of the community. They alert the auditors and police that many audit recommendations are based on crime-fighting folklores and exclude crime prevention and a vast array of services that impact upon the community. Beyond measures to make the police more efficient, the auditors seldom set goals and objectives for police effectiveness in improving public safety. Recommendations such as centralizing patrol operations and reducing the supervisor-officer ratio suggest that greater emphasis is on the economy and efficiency in managing police resources with little attention to the outcomes of such measures. This explains why the auditors, after establishing that the police organization is flawed, are not always able to design a replacement that embodies incentives for effective police management. Without a vision to realize external goals, a planned change effort may achieve outcomes different from those desired by the public (Klofas et al., 1990). With only objectives to accomplish higher efficiency, the police will only evaluate outcomes of their operations that are readily measurable or show favorable results (Hoos, 1983). To reduce such tendencies, a police audit should link all recommendations to desired goals or impacts external to the police whenever possible. The public serves as a critical resource to both auditors and police for understanding these goals and impacts in the audit implementation process.

Sixth, the planned change process involving police auditing requires implementation of audit recommendations along with efforts in organizational development. It should not be assumed that changes will occur naturally once solutions are developed and goals set. Changes should be planned together with preparations for change in order to reduce resistance to change. In this process, police executives may need to intensify their effort in educating or training police officers, align related policies and procedures with goals and objectives of the audit program, and modify certain organizational practices. These efforts should be introduced with the principle of maintaining a high morale and healthy organizational climate (Porter, Lawler, & Hackman, 1975) because an important purpose of organizational development is to increase the level of support for changes among organizational members (French, 1969). In police auditing, this means that police executives and rank-and-file officers should be involved in the audit to increase their sense of ownership of the audit program and ensure their commitment to changes according to the audit recommendations. They should be given as many opportunities as possible to participate in audit-related activities.

Many organizational development activities can be used to prepare an organization for change and reduce resistance to change. The police leaders, for example, may be able to link audit recommendations to police missions, values, culture, and purposes. According to Schein (1985), the routines of an organization and the work behaviors of its members are constrained by the collective value structure of the organization. To successfully implement audit recommendations, police executives should carefully examine whether the audit recommendations converge with or diverge from the value structure of their organization and devise implementation strategies accordingly. A police audit program, therefore, should not be viewed as an isolated event. Police leaders should seize this opportunity to shape their organizational culture and provide a clear, articulated vision of what the police stand for, a vision that embodies core values and purposes (Skolnick & Bayley, 1986).

Seventh, maintenance and monitoring activities must be carried out in order to keep the police from falling back to old routines and habits after the audit recommendations are implemented. As Ekblom and Pease (1995) indicated, protecting against implementation failure often requires evaluators to have monitoring systems in place to facilitate the implementation. For a city with a permanent police auditor or oversight body, the auditor and oversight body should have the authority and resources to ensure that recommended changes have been maintained. For a city without a permanent police auditor or oversight body, the audited police department should create a management committee to assume the role of maintaining the planned change. The city government should also set up an independent evaluation/audit team to be engaged in tracking and monitoring the audit-related activities. Serving as facilitators, moderators, and monitors, the management committee and/or evaluation/audit team should contribute positively to the audit program and ensure that key recommendations are not only implemented but maintained. The police executives and independent evaluators/auditors should reconvene every three to six months depending on the time frames for implementing the recommendations to assess the status of the audit program. To track progress, the parent government or an outside audit organization should also require that reports on the audit program be provided by the police department at regular intervals (Christopher Commission, 1999).

The final element in the model of planned change is outcome evaluation. Because internal or external action on major recommendations may take two to three years to complete due to budgetary constraints, union negotiations, and change of personnel, a strong need exists for a good audit follow-up system as well as a great deal of patience and perseverance. As a general rule, the auditors and/or evaluators should conduct the outcome evaluation in light of the goals set for the police to achieve higher efficiency and greater effectiveness with the completion of the audit program. If desired outcomes in the forms of higher efficiency and greater effectiveness are found, the audit recommendations and related planned change efforts should be maintained. If not, the audit recommendations and related planned change efforts may need to be reconsidered and recalibrated.

Outcome evaluation is an essential element in the model of planned change, but it cannot be applied to police auditing straightforwardly. Many difficulties in police performance measurement remain in evaluation of results (Audit Commission, 1990). Many of the benefits to be obtained from a police audit are intangible or qualitative in nature and cannot be fully evaluated (Brown et al., 1982). Some recommendations or guidelines to police departments can hardly be established along the lines that might be recognizable to middle managers as those in a commercial company (The Economist, 1990a). The impact of a police audit may be hard to discern, beyond the statistics the police and the auditing agency produce. Police audits do not always lend themselves to savings. Some recommendations may actually result in the expenditure of additional public funds designed to strengthen and improve a program or service or provide a needed but unavailable service. Police auditing may also fall into traps of statistical fallacy when police can raise their clearance rate by changing recording procedures and types of cases to be included (The Economist, 1990b). Audit evaluators, therefore, must endeavor to reduce or control these problems in order to have a meaningful evaluation.

In conclusion, police auditing can be regarded as a model of planned change with several essential and interrelated constructs. This model can be further refined and replicated with more police audit programs to be implemented and completed in the future. Police executives contemplating or responsible for planned changes should consider this model as well as its components as a viable approach to bringing about positive changes. As suggested in this chapter, a police audit can serve as an effective changing mechanism if police executives involved have a clear understanding of internal and external forces for change, are convinced that the organizational disequilibrium exists due to performance gaps and related organizational problems, engage in systematic data collection and rational decision-making, develop solutions by setting goals and objectives and searching for alternatives, implement planned changes along with efforts to develop their organization and reduce resistance to change, maintain and monitor the changes carefully as they are being brought about through the audit program, and evaluate audit outcomes systematically in light of goals set for achieving higher efficiency and greater effectiveness.

REFERENCES

Audit Commission of Local Authorities and the National Health Service in England and Wales. (1990). Effective policing: Performance review in police forces. *Police Papers, 8.*

Brown, R. E., Gallagher, T. P., & Williams, M. C. (1982). *Auditing performance in government: Concepts and cases.* New York: John Wiley.

Christopher Commission. (1999). Report of the Independent Commission on the Los Angeles Police Department. In L. K. Gaines & G. W. Cordner (Eds.), *Policing perspectives: An anthology.* Los Angeles: Roxbury.

The Economist. (1990a). Cooked. February 10, 314(7641), 56.

The Economist. (1990b). Footing the bill. February 10, 314(7641), 56 & 59.

Ekblom, P., & Pease, K. (1995). Evaluating crime prevention. In M. Tonry & D. P. Farrington (Eds.), *Building a safer society: Strategic approaches to crime prevention.* Chicago: University of Chicago Press.

French, W. L. (1969). Organizational development: Objectives, assumptions and strategies. *California Management Review, 12*(2), 23–35.

Hoos, I. R. (1983). *Systems analysis in public policy.* Los Angeles: University of California Press.

Ingram, F. (1990). The police service: Footing the bill. *Public Finance and Accountancy,* July 20, *11*(2).

Klofas, J., Stojkovic, S., & Kalinich, D. (1990). *Criminal justice organizations: Administration and management.* Pacific Grove, CA: Brooks/Cole.

Mackenzie, K. D. (1986). *Organizational design: The organizational audit and analysis technology.* Norwood, NJ: Ablex.

March, J. G., & Simon, H. A. (1958). *Organizations.* New York: John Wiley.

Poole, R. W. (1980). *Cutting back city hall.* New York: Universe Books.

Porter, L. W., Lawler, E. E., & Hackman, J. H. (1975). *Behavior in organizations.* New York: McGraw-Hill.

Schein, E. H. (1985). *Organizational culture and leadership.* San Francisco: Jossey-Bass.

Scott, R. (1987). *Organizations: Rational, natural, and open systems.* Englewood Cliffs, NJ: Prentice-Hall.

Skolnick, J. H., & Bayley, D. H. (1986). *The new blue line: Police innovation in six American cities.* New York: Free Press.

Walker, S. (2005). *The new world of police accountability.* Thousand Oaks, CA: Sage.

INDEX

201

Graded response. *See* Call grading

H

Hiring grant program, 7
Hoshin planning, 175
Hour of patrol, 69

I

I Search, 105
Illinois Legislative Audit Commission, 105
Illinois State Auditing Act, 106
Illinois State Office of the Auditor General, 105
Independent police auditor, 135–146; auditor qualifications, 136–138; functions, 138–140; office structure, 136–138; political and professional issues, 142–144; recommendations, 140–142; types of cases handled, 140
Injury, 70–71
Inspectorate of Constabulary, 90–91
Instrumental planning, 20
Intergovernmental Missing Child Recovery Act, 108
Internal and external auditors, 6
Internal controls, 8, 36, 42–43, 150
Internal structural change, 18
International Association of Chiefs of Police (IACP), 128, 129

J

Joint Legislative Oversight Committee of Arizona State, 111

L

Law Enforcement Agency Data System (LEADS), 108
Law enforcement grant, 80; Law Enforcement Assistance Administration (LEAA), 81–83
LEAA, 81–83; Management Advisory Task Force, 82
Legislative Commission on Expenditure Review (LCER), 84–86, 96–97

Local financial management, 115

M

Maintenance and monitoring, 197
Management audit, 39
Measure of effectiveness, 96, 107
Measurement criteria. *See* Performance criteria
Measurement validity and reliability, 67, 69
Metropolitan Police, 90, 103–105, 116–119
Mile patrolled, 69
Model of planned change, ix, 11, 25–26, 191–192, 198; *See also* Theoretical model of police auditing
Municipal Police Training Council (MPTC), 96, 99–100

N

National Audit Office, 90, 92, 102–105, 116–117, 119
New Jersey Law Enforcement Study Commission, 168
New Jersey Local Government Budget Review Program, 167
New Jersey State Attorney General, 166, 169 New Jersey State Police, 167, 186
New York City Police Department, 97, 99
New York State Police, 84, 86, 97, 99

O

Office of the Independent Police Auditor. *See* Independent police auditor
Office of Management and Budget (OMB), 33; circular, 83
Omnibus Crime Control and Safe Streets Act, 83
Operational audit, 39
Operational definition, 164
Organizational audit, 6
Organizational development, 18, 23–24, 25, 196, 197
Organizational disequilibrium, 18, 193, 199
Outcome evaluation, 150–151, 156–162, 178–179, 198; validity of, 143–144
Oversight responsibilities, vii, 5